THE

ENGLISH

LIBRARY

General Editor JAMES SUTHERLAND

Emeritus Professor of English Literature
University College, London

THE
METAPHYSICAL
POETS

Edited by
MARGARET WILLY

UNIVERSITY OF SOUTH CAROLINA PRESS
Columbia, S.C.

© Margaret Willy 1971

First published 1971 in Great Britain by
EDWARD ARNOLD (PUBLISHERS) LTD.
41 Maddox Street, London W1R 0AN

And in the United States of America by the
UNIVERSITY OF SOUTH CAROLINA PRESS
Columbia, S.C. 29208

International Standard Book Number: 0–87249–232–X
Library of Congress Catalog Card Number: 70–161618

Suggested Library of Congress classification furnished by
McKissick Memorial Library of the University of South Carolina:
PR1205.W

General Preface

THE design of this series is to present fully annotated selections from English literature which will, it is hoped, prove satisfactory both in their breadth and their depth. To achieve this, some of the volumes have been planned so as to provide a varied selection from the poetry or prose of a limited period, which is both long enough to have developed a literary movement, and short enough to allow for adequate representation of the chief writers and of the various cross-currents within the movement. Examples of such periods are the late seventeenth century and the early eighteenth century. In other volumes the principle of selection is to present a literary kind (e.g. satirical poetry, the literary ballad). Here it is possible to cover a longer period without sacrificing the unified and comprehensive treatment which is the governing idea for the whole series. Other volumes, again, are designed to present a group of writers who form some kind of "school" (e.g. the Elizabethan sonneteers, the followers of Ben Jonson), or who were closely enough linked for their work to be brought together (e.g. the poetry of Johnson and Goldsmith).

Each volume has a full critical introduction. Headnotes, a special feature of this series, provide relevant background and critical comment for the individual poems and prose pieces. The footnotes are for the most part explanatory, giving as briefly as possible information about persons, places, allusions of one kind or another, the meaning of words, etc., which the twentieth-century reader is likely to require. Each selection aims at providing examples of the best work of the authors represented, but it is hoped that the inclusion of some less familiar pieces not available in any other collection will widen the reader's experience and enjoyment of the literature under review. The series is intended for use in universities and the upper forms of schools.

In this comprehensive selection of Metaphysical poetry, Margaret Willy has naturally given most space to John Donne; but Herbert, Crashaw, Marvell, Henry Vaughan and Traherne are also represented by some of their best and most characteristic poems. The other poets included range from Ralegh and Wotton at one end of the Metaphysical cycle to Cleveland and Cowley at the other. In her critical introduction Miss Willy examines the main features of Metaphysical poetry, and also draws attention to the numerous affinities between the world of Donne and his contemporaries and that of our own day. The similarity of the human situation in the two periods gives this poetry a peculiar relevance for the twentieth-century reader.

A special feature of this edition is Miss Willy's full explanatory commentary. The Metaphysical poets present many difficulties for the modern reader. In their poems, as Dr. Johnson remarked, "Nature and art are ransacked for illustrations, comparisons, and allusions"; and if these were not always easily comprehensible to seventeenth-century readers, they are often still less intelligible three hundred years later. Metaphysical poetry, too, is marked by what Miss Willy calls an "elliptical economy" of expression, and, as often as not, by "a subtle, close-knit and often paradoxical argument"; it abounds in conceits, and in the startling juxtaposition of remote and apparently disconnected ideas. In her headnotes and in her running commentary Miss Willy's aim has been to supply the reader with the sort of information he needs for a full understanding and enjoyment of the poems she has chosen, and, where necessary, with an exposition of passages in which the meaning is complex and subject to different interpretations.

Contents

Acknowledgements

The editor and publisher would like to thank the Clarendon Press, Oxford, for permission to reproduce copyright material from the editions listed in the Bibliography.

Introduction

WE in our time have witnessed a major resurgence of interest in the work of the seventeenth-century Metaphysical poets. Grierson's edition of Donne appeared as early as 1912, and more recently the *Songs and Sonnets* and *Divine Poems* have been edited by Helen Gardner. L. C. Martin's collected edition of Vaughan (1914) and of Crashaw (1927) were both reissued in 1957. The collected poems of Herbert edited by F. E. Hutchinson have several times been reprinted since their appearance in 1941, and Dobell's work on Traherne early in the century has been followed by H. M. Margoliouth's two-volume collected edition in 1958. Margoliouth also edited the works of Marvell in 1927 (reprinted 1952). Essays by T. S. Eliot on the Metaphysical and Caroline poets were powerfully influential in this general reassessment during the nineteen-twenties, and have been followed by the valuable critical work of scholars like Joan Bennett, J. B. Leishman, Evelyn M. Simpson on Donne, Ruth C. Wallerstein on Crashaw, Rosemond Tuve on Herbert, and various volumes by Louis L. Martz in America and Mario Praz in Italy. There have also been a number of full-scale biographies —Leishman's of Donne, F. E. Hutchinson's of Vaughan, Pierre Legouis's of Marvell, and lives of Traherne by Gladys I. Wade and K. W. Salter. The many anthologies have ranged from Grierson's *Metaphysical Lyrics and Poems of the Seventeenth Century* in 1921 to Helen Gardner's *The Metaphysical Poets*, first published in 1957. And throughout the poetry of our time, beginning with Hopkins at the end of the nineteenth century and continuing with Eliot, Yeats (who affirmed that "I may dine at journey's end/With Landor and with Donne"), and innumerable lesser writers, echoes of both the mood and the manner of the seventeenth-century Metaphysicals have abounded. There is not space here for any detailed exploration of various striking parallels between men's habits of mind then and now, and their modes of expressing these. It does, however, reward close study to compare such aspects as the common use of colloquial idiom, "contemporary" imagery and metaphysical wit; the shared awareness of the inter-relationship between the life of man and the universe;

and the similarities between Donne and Yeats in their treatment of the theme of love.

What is the reason for the appeal to us of these poets writing three centuries ago, who were attacked by the critics of the Augustan Age which succeeded them and were largely unappreciated—with the notable exceptions of Coleridge and, later, Browning—during the nineteenth century? Basically it seems to spring from certain affinities between conditions of life and thought in Jacobean and Caroline England and those we ourselves have been experiencing during the past seventy years. The seventeenth century was an age of transition between an outgrown old order and a rebellious new, characterized by a spirit of intense intellectual and scientific curiosity and the many practical discoveries which resulted. Geographically the late Elizabethan voyages by men like Gilbert, Davis, Drake and Ralegh, as well as those of the great European explorers, had opened up worlds unrealized; and these new wonders on earth were matched by others no less astonishing in the heavens. The Ptolemaic system of astronomy, which held that the earth was the centre of the universe and that the sun and planets moved round it, had been accepted throughout the Middle Ages. It was not until the sixteenth century that this was challenged by Copernicus, who affirmed that the planets, including the earth, moved in orbit round the sun at the centre: a theory confirmed by Kepler's formulation of his laws of planetary motion. For seventeenth-century men such things were shaking the whole foundations of their earlier conception of the workings of the macrocosm; and at the same time their knowledge of the "little world" of the human body was being steadily enlarged by the findings of contemporary anatomists. As Donne put it in "An Anatomie of the World. The first Anniversary":

> And new Philosophy calls all in doubt,
> The Element of fire is quite put out;
> The Sun is lost, and th'earth, and no man's wit
> Can well direct him where to look for it.
> And freely men confess that this world's spent,
> When in the Planets, and the Firmament
> They seek so many new; then see that this
> Is crumbled out again to his Atomies.
> 'Tis all in pieces, all coherence gone;
> All just supply, and all Relation . . .
> Man hath weav'd out a net, and this net thrown
> Upon the Heavens, and now they are his own . . .

Thou know'st how wan a Ghost this our world is:
And learn'st thus much by our Anatomy,
That it should more affright, than pleasure thee.

and in "Of the Progresse of the Soule. The second Anniversary":

Thou art too narrow, wretch, to comprehend
Even thyself: yea though thou wouldst but bend
To know thy body. Have not all souls thought
For many ages, that our body is wrought
Of Air, and Fire, and other Elements?
And now they think of new ingredients,
And one Soul thinks one, and another way
Another thinks, and 'tis an even lay.

Something of the sense of bewildered uncertainty and doubt expressed here at the teaching of the "new" scientists and philosophers, so swiftly displacing the accustomed shape of the medieval world-picture, must at some time have been experienced by each one of us living in a similar period of flux and rapid change. Ours is the century of the internal combustion engine, the first aeroplane, the growth of mass communication by radio and television and of mass destruction of our own kind by the high-explosive bomb; of the splitting of the atom, and the first landing on the moon. It has also witnessed a pervasive questioning of all traditional assumptions and ideas, including the Christian faith still shared as a common background of belief by men in Donne's day. Human curiosity in the seventeenth century worked, as it has in the twentieth, in the context of violent social and political upheaval. The Golden Age of the first Queen Elizabeth was followed by the troubled years after the Essex Rebellion and the Queen's death, culminating in the conflagration of civil war. Three hundred years later the seeming stability of material prosperity and expansion in Victorian and Edwardian England was swept away for ever by the first war of this century, succeeded by two decades of uneasy peace which led inevitably to the second. It is small wonder that in both instances the "new" poetry which emerged not only reflected men's response to a disintegrating established order, but challenged the poetic "voice" which had been its expression. T. S. Eliot and Ezra Pound were reacting against the outworn conventions of the Georgians who preceded them as vigorously as were Donne and his fellows against the Petrarchan tradition predominant in the latter half of the sixteenth century. It is interesting to compare the antagonism their reaction aroused. Johnson's complaint that the seventeenth-century Metaphysical poets were "always analytick" and "broke every image into fragments" was couched in analogous terms to that levelled by at least one reviewer of Eliot's "The Love Song of J. Alfred Prufrock" when it appeared in 1917.

It can be seen, then, that the sympathy we feel with the Metaphysical poets of the seventeenth century is something far more compelling than any mere superficial attraction to their attitudes and techniques. It is rooted deep in social and historical circumstance: in conditions which have produced climates of thought and responses to experience in many ways essentially similar.

Of all the Metaphysicals it was John Donne (1572–1631), their acknowledged leader, who had his finger most surely on the pulse of awareness in this age of change, and who most forcefully embodies its main characteristics. He started out as a student of the Inns of Court, one of the gay and keen-witted young gallants of Shakespeare's London: according to Walton "a great visitor of ladies, and a great frequenter of plays". He later became secretary to Sir Thomas Egerton, Keeper of the Great Seal. At that time he was writing love poetry full of the impudence and flippant cynicism which, as Grierson notes, very much resembles the utterances of one of the young men in an early Shakespeare comedy. This fashionable pose was a conscious reaction against conventional ideas of fidelity ("I can love any," declared Donne, "so she be not true") and the whole image of the pining lover, prostrate and spurned at the feet of his disdainful mistress, which had been celebrated by the earlier Elizabethan song-writers and sonneteers. Shakespeare wrote in a similar mood, mocking the Petrarchan lover's "woeful ballad/Made to his mistress' eyebrow", in the downright affirmation in Sonnet 130 that his own "mistress' eyes are nothing like the sun", nor did various other parts of her anatomy resemble the coral, snow and roses of customary "false compare". The self-consciously defiant disenchantment of Donne's early love poetry made an impact on his younger contemporaries which may clearly be seen in the work of Court poets like Carew and Suckling.

Donne outgrew the clever ingenuities of wit for their own sake to become, in his maturity, the greatest poet of human and the most eloquent and impassioned apologist of divine love in the language. A keenly ambitious man disappointed in his hopes of worldly preferment by an imprudent marriage (see footnote to l. 3 of "The Canonization", p. 34), he finally turned from thoughts of the secular advancement which had failed him to the permanent values of the spiritual life. He was ordained in 1615, two years before the death of his greatly loved wife, which strengthened the wholeness of his surrender to religion. From the tensions imposed by his calling upon a strongly sensual temperament flowed the power and passion of his divine poems. A similar conflict between worldliness and religious vocation characterized the life and work of George Herbert (see notes to "Affliction", "The Collar" and "The Flower", pp. 87-98). It is worth noting, in viewing Metaphysical poetry as the direct product of the age in which its writers lived, that all of them were practically involved in the world of their time and experienced in its ways. Donne himself in his youth sailed in the two expeditions of Essex to Cadiz and to the Islands in the war against Spain. Andrew Marvell was a man of affairs—assistant to Milton in the Latin Secretaryship, Member of Parliament, and a spirited champion of constitutional liberties. Most of the secular and Court poets—Cleveland, Cowley, Davenant, Waller, Suckling and Lovelace—were committed to the Royalist cause and actively engaged in the great struggle of the mid-century between King and Parliament. The religious Metaphysicals too were in no sense cloistered recluses. Donne's experience of secular activities, as we have seen, had been rich and varied before his appointment in 1621 as Dean of St. Paul's. Herbert before his ordination was one of the most brilliant and promising young men of his day who hoped to make a career at Court. Traherne, presented to a country living in 1657, went ten years later to London to work at the Court as chaplain to Sir Orlando Bridgeman, Lord Keeper of the Great Seal. Crashaw, after his ejection by the Parliamentary Commissioners from the "little contentfull kingdom" of his Fellowship at Peterhouse, lived abroad in Holland and Paris and finally died in Italy. Vaughan practised for many years as a doctor of medicine. All experienced the inner realities of the spiritual life they so vividly recorded amid the practical daily ones of the world they inhabited.

What are the main characteristics of seventeenth-century Metaphysical poetry? It is "metaphysical", says Grierson in his 1912 edition of Donne, "not only in the sense of being erudite and witty, but in the proper sense of being reflective and philosophical". He defines metaphysical poetry in its fullest interpretation as work "inspired by a philosophical conception of the universe and the role assigned to the human spirit in the great drama of existence". In their "imaginative apprehension of emotional identity in diverse experience", the great metaphysical poets like Lucretius, Dante and Goethe perceived a harmonious universal pattern and plan. Donne differed from them in that acute awareness of disharmony and doubt which arose from the play of his restless, probing intelligence upon the changing world around him, with its conflicts between the old and the new learning. Yet of all the seventeenth-century poets he, both in his familiarity with the tenets of medieval Scholasticism and his view of the significance of human experience in relation to the universe by which it is enlarged and dignified, is in the truest sense "metaphysical". What might be called a cosmic curiosity characterizes his passionate investigation of the nature of life in man the microcosm—especially in its intensest forms, love and religion—as it echoes and is echoed by the macrocosm around it. Dryden in 1693 had said that Donne "affects the metaphysics"; but the term "Metaphysical" as applied to the work of Donne and his fellows was first employed in the following century when Johnson attacked them in his life of Cowley. It has continued to describe their distinctive qualities better than any other

One of the most obvious of these is the concentration of language achieved by an elliptical economy, a syntax sometimes tortuously complex, and the development of a subtle, close-knit and often paradoxical argument. The taste for dialectic and paradox derived from medieval poetry, and the epigrammatic intensity ("The metaphysical poem," says Helen Gardner, "is an expanded epigram") from the influence of the classical epigram which can be most clearly seen in the work of Crashaw. The metaphysical blend of reason with imagination—what Grierson calls "passionate ratiocination"—often employs the vehicle of an extended image or sustained line of argument so densely packed in texture that it demands the utmost alertness of attention in the reader. But at its best the effort is repaid, as in the mature work of Donne, where thought is invariably charged with feeling both authentic and deeply experienced. As Eliot said, "A thought, to Donne, was an experience; it modified his sensibility." Metaphysical poetry could, in fact, be defined as "feeling thought": the product of thinking with the heart, feeling with the mind—of stirring the emotions by first stimulating the intellect. Donne himself epitomized the process in his allusion in "The Blossome" to his "naked thinking heart . . . which lov'st to be/Subtile to plague thy selfe".

Coming after the melodious songs and sonnets of the Elizabethans, the versification of Metaphysical poetry is often distinctly rough, angular, even harsh: prickly as a cactus by contrast with the flowers of poetic eloquence which had already begun to wither. The Metaphysical poet deliberately rejected the formal metrical smoothness and preconceived poetic patterns of the past in order to allow the requirements of each particular poem to dictate its own stanza-form and rhyme-scheme. Not only Donne, but Herbert, Vaughan and Traherne (who, incidentally, never used the same verse-form twice) placed great importance on the part played by the pattern of the poem on the printed page in conveying its total meaning. All em-

ployed lines of varying lengths which, as Grierson says, "bend and crack the
metrical pattern to the rhetoric of direct and vehement utterance . . .
striving to find a rhythm which will express the passionate fullness of . . .
mind, the flux and reflux of . . . moods". Ben Jonson commented less
sympathetically when he declared that "for not keeping of accent [Donne]
deserved hanging", while Dryden found him wanting in "sweetness and
strength of versification".

Another of Dryden's complaints was that Donne lacked "dignity of
expression". This allusion was to the use of that colloquial idiom which,
after the poetic abstractions of the past, has such a vivid and exciting
individuality, a quality both intensely personal and essentially dramatic.
Donne and his fellows were, after all, writing in the great age of the English
drama, as distinct from that of the lyric before it and the one which followed
of descriptive and reflective poetry and of the essay and the novel. Their
employment of speech rhythms and colloquial diction was as much a
reflection of this as their omnivorous appetite for experience and the
sensibility which absorbed and re-interpreted their wide learning. In contrast
with the courtly chivalry of the Petrarchan tradition, Donne's forms of
address are often audaciously familiar. His "Busie old foole, unruly Sunne . . .
Sawcy pedantique wretch" rudely displaces Phoebus riding in his fiery car
or the "golden globe incontinent" of his predecessors. The sighs and adora-
tion of the Elizabethan lover give way to the aggressive abruptness of such
openings as "For Godsake hold your tongue, and let me love", or "So, so,
breake off this last lamenting kisse". The raw realism of the adjective
"spongy" for a weeping woman's eyes ("The Indifferent") or of the verb
"snorted" in a love poem ("The Good-morrow") are as defiantly and
daringly down-to-earth as many of the images expressing a similar reaction
in the 'twenties and 'thirties of this century against the sentimental poeticisms
of the Georgians.

Central to the nature of Metaphysical poetry is its concept of wit. To
Donne and his followers the aim of the conceit was basically different from
its mainly ornamental use by the Elizabethans. The seventeenth-century
Metaphysical poet saw wit as no frivolous decoration, but as intrinsic to a
poem's meaning, and compatible with the most sober and solemn purpose
(see notes to "A Hymne to God the Father", pp. 84–5) as a powerful method
of heightening its intensity. Through—in Eliot's phrase—"constantly
amalgamating disparate experience" and linking apparently incongruous
objects and forms of existence, he sought to establish the underlying unity
of all phenomena. "Nature and art", as Johnson observed, "are ransacked
for illustrations, comparisons, and allusions." Donne and his contemporaries

employed imagery mainly of two kinds. Erudite and recondite analogies were drawn from classical myth (like the Phoenix legend in "The Canonization", p. 33), the definitions of the medieval Schoolmen (see footnote to ll. 19–21 of "The Good-morrow", p. 13), from theology, alchemy, mathematics and the significance of numbers, astrology, anatomy and medicine, and the law. At the other extreme, the homeliest and most boldly prosaic imagery is constantly employed by Herbert and often by Donne. The latter speaks in "Twicknam Garden" of "the spider love", and devotes a poem to the flea whose body which unites the blood of lover and mistress is thus their "mariage bed, and mariage temple". In "The Dissolution" he likens the passage of souls after death to the flight of bullets. This was the kind of image which Johnson attacked as the Metaphysicals' "slender conceits and laboured particularities". Admittedly the extravagant or fantastic metaphor will sometimes plunge into a bathos (most notably in Crashaw) which justifies Johnson's criticism of "heterogeneous ideas . . . yoked by violence together". But at their best there is in these startling analogies and juxtapositions, with their alliance of physical and spiritual, prosaic and poetic, the trivial and the tremendous, an impact of aptness and complete rightness. The swift brilliance of their illumination, the freshness of the emotional and imaginative intuitions they yield, do in fact produce precisely those effects of "sudden astonishment" followed by "rational admiration" which Johnson denies them. In the hands of its masters the metaphysical conceit transcends a mere clever cerebral exercise in verbal ingenuity through having been, in Grierson's words, "purified by the passionate heat of the poet's dramatic imagination"; and thus commands in us far more than detached appreciation of the kind of originality of which Johnson accused them—the "wish . . . only to say what they hoped had never been said before".

Reflecting the interests of an era of scientific speculation and invention and geographical discovery, seventeenth-century Metaphysical poetry abounds in the kind of simile and metaphor calculated to catch the contemporary reader on the quick of imagination. Donne's sea-discoverers, cosmographers, maps, latitude and longitude, globes and hemispheres, will be encountered in this anthology; and in "A Valediction: forbidding mourning" he uses the action of a pair of compasses to illustrate in minute specific detail the experience of the souls of parted lovers. Marvell's "The Definition of Love" (p. 72) draws on both the parallel lines of geometry and contemporary notions of astrology. Such images are echoed in our own century by the industrial and economic metaphors of poetry in a machine age obsessed with money: "thoughts like sailplanes", "history's high-tension", a "depth-charge of grief", "the dynamo of summer"; "the dreamer's mad/Inflated currency", "the tyrant's dishonoured cheque", "imagination's slump", and so on.

The subjects and themes of seventeenth-century Metaphysical poetry are the perennial ones. Human love is, as it always will be, a main preoccupation; but the stimulating originality lies in its treatment. There is now to be observed a broadening of range in the lover's moods and attitudes, a conception of passion more varied, complex and profound, and a depth of psychological insight into its contradictions and inconsistencies, unhinted at in those whom Grierson aptly describes as the "pipers of Petrarch's woes". The rebellion of Donne and his contemporaries against those threadbare conventions of sentiment and diction resulted in a portrayal of love informed by a powerful realism never before achieved in the English lyric. Their poems are at once more vigorous in their response to the woman's acceptance or rejection of her lover, and more full-blooded and feeling even at their most argumentative. They have a personal quality, a human warmth, which invalidate Dryden's complaint that Donne "perplexes the minds of the fair sex with nice speculations of philosophy, when he should engage their hearts, and entertain them with the softnesses of love". The influence of the fashionable disenchantment of his early addresses to his "profane mistresses" has already been noted. In his later, greater ones, some of which may be read in these pages, love between man and woman has become the means of the individual's highest self-realization. They express a conviction of the supremacy of love over every other human experience; a searching preoccupation with the relationship between senses and spirit; and a perception that the completest union—the recurring idea of "oneness" of being is perhaps the most memorable theme in Donne's mature love poems —may be achieved only by way of the physical act. "Love must not be," he says in "Aire and Angels", "but take a body too"; and "The Exstasie" is his fullest exploration of this recognition that "soule into the soule may flow,/ Though it to body first repaire".

A pervasive awareness of the fact of death as a constant shadow over present joys was inseparable in many of the Metaphysical poets from their experience of love. Marvell's "To his Coy Mistress" is the supreme expression in seventeenth-century poetry of the vulnerability of love by the trespass of time. Donne himself was obsessed by the idea of the loss of his love through death. Like Webster in Eliot's "Whispers of Immortality", he saw everywhere "the skull beneath the skin". In earlier poems like "The Apparition", "The Legacie", "The Dampe", the subject is treated more lightly, in a quizzical, ironical or frankly mocking vein. But in such magnificent later pieces as "The Dissolution", "The Relique", "The Funerall" and "The Anniversarie", Donne probes the mysteries of love and death at a much profounder level. Others beside him—most notably Henry King in "The Exequy"—explored with moving eloquence the question of whether the spirit of love, unconfined by time and mortality, may be enduring enough to defy the corruption of the grave. It is such utterances as these which, taken with Donne's greatest love poems, provide the unassailable answer to Johnson's assertion that "Their courtship was void of fondness and their lamentation of sorrow".

In all the intellectual and political turmoil of the seventeenth century, the Christian faith was still rooted deep enough to withstand the tides of insecurity and change. This is perhaps the greatest point of separation between Donne's century and our own. Donne apprehended the love of God as essentially the same kind of mystical experience as that of human passion at its highest—when, as in "The Exstasie" and most of the poems in the first section here, sense is sublimated in a total fusion of two souls. Donne's perception of the relationship between human and divine love may also be seen in the imagery and ideas of many of his contemporaries. Herbert frequently addresses God in the intimate tone of a lover: "Ah my deare,/I cannot look on thee" ("Love"). To Vaughan, God was the "first love" or "early love" to whom he had been close in childhood and from whom he was now separated by sin (see notes to "The Retreate", pp. 119–21): the Bridegroom of "The World", preparing a place for his mystical marriage with the soul, his bride. Erotic imagery abounds in the work of Crashaw, who writes of the joys of the soul who "shall discover . . . /How many heavens at once it is,/To have a God become her lover" ("On a prayer booke sent to Mrs. M. R."). Donne himself uses sexual imagery in a religious context most overtly of all, as in "Batter my heart, three person'd God" (pp. 79–80) and the close of the Holy Sonnet beginning "Show me deare Christ, thy spouse". The conflicts in his turbulent nature were never finally subdued; so it is not really surprising that his later spiritual hunger should so often have been communicated in terms of the earlier one which had led him to it. His divine poems present a unique blend of ardour and asceticism, a relationship of his whole being with God as passionately personal as with any of his human loves. The doubts, fears and agonized sense of sin they express charge Donne's striving towards holiness and supplications for the love and mercy of God with a tormented intensity which recalls the spiritual struggles of Gerard Manley Hopkins two-and-a-half centuries later. (There are striking echoes of Herbert, too, in the work of Hopkins: see notes to "The Flower", pp. 94–5.)

Abraham Cowley, who died in 1667, over thirty years after Donne, was the last considerable poet to write in the Metaphysical manner. Already in his work, however, the driving imaginative force of the great Metaphysicals was spent (see headnote to "The Spring", p. 66); and his poetry exhibits what Eliot called "a kind of emotional drought, and a verbal ingenuity which, having no great depth of feeling to work upon, tends towards corruption of language". Wit, in Cowley, remains an intellectual exercise: a fanciful or decorative embellishment uninformed by that intensity of the passionate imagination which transmutes mere thought and which achieved, in the work of Donne and Marvell, so potent a fusion of reason and feeling. The predominance of reason in his poems made Cowley more congenial than his fellows to Johnson's age of "rational admiration", in which Pope condemned the "glitt'ring thoughts" of the Metaphysicals and Addison their "Fashion of false Wit". A later century may, however, find the most notable feature of Cowley's work the illustration it provides of what happens when a poetic fashion outlives its vitalizing creative impetus. He is no less representative of a major movement in decline than are the Georgian poets of 1912–22 who spoke with the dying voice of the great nineteenth- century Romantics.

I: POEMS OF LOVE AND DEATH

John Donne

THE GOOD-MORROW

THIS poem was published (like the others by Donne in this section) in *Songs and Sonnets* in 1633. Reacting against the Petrarchan fashion of adoring a remote, disdainful mistress (see Introduction, p. 4), Donne presents a far more realistic and complex view of passion as a mutual exchange between the sexes. He addresses the woman with vigorous directness, and with a defiance of conventional poetic diction in his calculated use in the first verse of the audaciously prosaic verb "snorted". The intensity of the relationship which can concentrate a world in "one little roome", and Donne's conviction that this transcends every other human adventure, are powerfully communicated through images from the late Elizabethan voyages of discovery. In the last verse, where he likens the lovers' eyes to hemispheres and introduces the further "contemporary" analogy of the simple and compound substances in the universe, human love finally acquires a cosmic significance.

> I wonder by my troth, what thou, and I
> Did, till we lov'd? were we not wean'd till then?
> But suck'd on countrey pleasures, childishly?
> Or snorted we in the seaven sleepers den?
> 5   'Twas so; But this, all pleasures fancies bee.
> If ever any beauty I did see,
>   Which I desir'd, and got, 'twas but a dreame of thee.
>
> And now good morrow to our waking soules,
> Which watch not one another out of feare;
> 10 For love, all love of other sights controules,
> And makes one little roome, an every where.

Let sea-discoverers to new worlds have gone,
Let Maps to others, worlds on worlds have showne,
Let us possesse one world, each hath one, and is one.

15 My face in thine eye, thine in mine appeares,
And true plaine hearts doe in the faces rest,
Where can we finde two better hemisphaeres
Without sharpe North, without declining West?
What ever dyes, was not mixt equally;
20 If our two loves be one, or thou and I
Love so alike, that none doe slacken, none can die.

3 *countrey pleasures:* rustic or simple, compared with the refinements of City or Court. Perhaps, too (as in Hamlet's reference to "country matters", III, ii, 117), mere enjoyment of sex contrasted with the maturity of love.

4 *the seaven sleepers den:* According to legend seven young Christian men of Ephesus took refuge in a cave during the persecution of Diocletian, and were walled up by their pursuers. They fell into a miraculous sleep, and were discovered alive almost two centuries later.

5 *But this:* except for, compared with, this.

13-14 *Let Maps . . . is one:* i.e. Let maps reveal "worlds on worlds" (therefore probably maps of the heavens, showing new spheres) to other people; but let us—each of whom inhabits, and is, a little world—possess the single world created by our love.

18 *Without sharpe North . . . West?:* i.e. Our love can feel neither the coldness of the North nor the sun's decline in the West.

19-21 *What ever dyes . . . none can die:* The lovers' oneness of ll. 13-14 is affirmed more forcefully still. Everything that dies contains unequal contraries (the idea of corruption and dissolution occurring where contrariety exists echoes a passage in the *Summa Theologica* of Aquinas). Only those simple substances which are single and unmixed (literally "one"), or compounds whose elements contain no inequalities or contraries, as in the fusion of two loves which are exactly "alike", can be indestructible.

THE SUNNE RISING

HERE Donne reiterates his belief in the sovereignty of love over every human and natural activity and form of existence. Its boundlessness defies the limits of both time and space; its comprehensiveness embraces all the richness of the earth's resources and of man's worldly power. Exploring these twin themes in a series of brilliant paradoxes which relate the experience of lovers to the daily duties of the sun, this poem exemplifies at its most satisfying the metaphysical fusion of wit and passion. Again current poetic convention is boldly challenged by the speech rhythms and the colloquial tone in which the maker of time is rebuked with disrespectful familiarity as an ancient busybody, "unruly" in interfering where it has no right and "pedantic" in its insistence on rule and habit. The opening mood of impudent irreverence passes imperceptibly into the high seriousness and lyrical intensity of the conclusion.

> Busie old foole, unruly Sunne,
> Why dost thou thus,
> Through windowes, and through curtaines call on us?
> Must to thy motions lovers seasons run?
> 5   Sawcy pedantique wretch, goe chide
> Late schoole boyes, and sowre prentices,
> Goe tell Court-huntsmen, that the King will ride,
> Call countrey ants to harvest offices;
> Love, all alike, no season knowes, nor clyme,
> 10 Nor houres, dayes, months, which are the rags of time.
>
> Thy beames, so reverend, and strong
> Why shouldst thou thinke?
> I could eclipse and cloud them with a winke,
> But that I would not lose her sight so long:
> 15   If her eyes have not blinded thine,
> Looke, and to morrow late, tell mee,
> Whether both the'India's of spice and Myne
> Be where thou leftst them, or lie here with mee.
> Aske for those Kings whom thou saw'st yesterday,
> 20 And thou shalt heare, All here in one bed lay.
>
> She'is all States, and all Princes, I,
> Nothing else is.
> Princes doe but play us; compar'd to this,
> All honor's mimique; All wealth alchimie.
> 25   Thou sunne art halfe as happy'as wee,

In that the world's contracted thus;
Thine age askes ease, and since thy duties bee
To warme the world, that's done in warming us.
Shine here to us, and thou art every where;
30   This bed thy center is, these walls, thy spheare.

7 *that the King will ride:* This topical allusion to James I's addiction to hunting shows that the poem was written after 1603.

8 *Call countrey ants . . . offices:* i.e. Call farm-workers to their harvesting duties.

9 *Love, all alike:* Love, which is unchanging.

10 *rags of time:* i.e. time's tattered clothing, or the shreds—hours, days, months—into which it is torn up (cf. the same phrase, referring to the mercy of God, in Donne's Christmas sermon of 1624).

14 *But . . . long:* i.e. except that I would not lose sight of her for even so short a time.

17 *both the'India's . . . Myne:* i.e. the East Indies, famous for spices, and the West Indies, famous for gold. Donne frequently refers in his poems, sermons and letters to mines, the perfumes and spices of the East, and the gold of the West Indies.

18 *where thou leftst them:* on your last journey round the earth.

22-3 *Nothing . . . play us:* i.e. Nothing else exists. Princes only act our reality.

24 *mimique:* mere imitation; *alchimie:* counterfeit (cf. Habington, p. 50, l. 12: "And grant all gold's not Alchimie").

25 *halfe as happy' as wee:* because the sun's is solitary, theirs the shared happiness of two.

26 *contracted:* concentrated.

27 *Thine age askes ease:* In Ovid, *Met.* ii, 385-7, Phoebus complains of his endless unrequited labour.

29 *thou art every where:* echoing the thought of l. 20. Also cf. "The Good-morrow", l. 11: "And makes one little roome, an every where".

30 *This bed . . . spheare:* i.e. This bed is the centre of your orbit, the earth round which you must revolve, and these walls its boundary.

A VALEDICTION: OF WEEPING

T. S. ELIOT notes in this poem, written when Donne was about to go overseas, the "development by rapid association of thought which requires

considerable agility on the part of the reader". Yet a genuine depth and
poignancy of emotion are conveyed by the succession of ideas which spring
from the central conceit of the tears of each lover bearing the reflection of
the other. At first the speaker justifies his own grief at parting, but when his
mistress also begins to weep he dissuades her, seeing in her tears and sighs a
premonition of future disaster (the idea of himself, like his reflection,
"drown'd in a transparent teare" is repeated in the poem "Witchcraft by a
Picture"). The cosmological analogies of worlds, moon and seas both
enlarge and intensify the experience of love in man, the little world.
Donne brings together here several of his favourite and most fruitful images.
The figure of coinage (ll. 3-4) is also used in l. 7 of "The Canonization",
and that of the geographer's globe and maps in the second stanza of "Hymne
to God my God, in my sicknesse". The metaphor of lovers' eyes as globes
or worlds reflecting the face of the other echoes the "hemispheares" of
"The Good-morrow" (ll. 15-18) and the image of eyes as "mirrors" in
ll. 41-2 of "The Canonization". For extended and illuminating discussion
of this poem see K. W. Gransden, *John Donne* ("Men and Books" series,
1954), and William Empson, *Seven Types of Ambiguity*.

       Let me powre forth
My teares before thy face, whil'st I stay here,
For thy face coines them, and thy stampe they beare,
And by this Mintage they are something worth,
5   For thus they bee
       Pregnant of thee;
Fruits of much griefe they are, emblemes of more,
When a teare falls, that thou falls which it bore,
So thou and I are nothing then, when on a divers shore.

10   On a round ball
A workeman that hath copies by, can lay
An Europe, Afrique, and an Asia,
And quickly make that, which was nothing, *All*,
       So doth each teare,
15   Which thee doth weare,
A globe, yea world by that impression grow,
Till thy teares mixt with mine doe overflow
This world, by waters sent from thee, my heaven dissolved so.

O more than Moone,
20 Draw not up seas to drowne me in thy spheare,
Weepe me not dead, in thine armes, but forbeare
To teach the sea, what it may doe too soone;
Let not the winde
Example finde,
25 To doe me more harme, than it purposeth;
Since thou and I sigh one anothers breath,
Who e'r sighes most, is cruellest, and hasts the others death.

2 *whil'st I stay here:* while I am still here with you.

3–6 *For thy face . . . thee:* i.e. For the sight of your face makes ("coins") my tears, and they reflect your image, and thus are given value because they are full of your significance.

7–9 *emblemes of more . . . shore:* i.e. because when a tear falls, that particular you ("that thou") which it reflected falls too and dissolves, and thus we also become nothing when parted by the sea.

10–13 *On a round ball . . . :* All: i.e. On a blank terrestrial globe a workman who has copies of the world beside him can, by pasting his map of the continents upon it, quickly make all out of nothing (cf. the quotation from a sermon in the headnote to "Hymne to God my God, in my sicknesse", p. 82).

14–18 *So doth . . . dissolved so:* i.e. In the same way each of my tears which bears your reflection is transformed by it into a world, until your tears mingling with mine overflow this world. "My heaven" may refer simultaneously to his mistress and to his happiness; so that by weeping she destroys (dissolves) both, and causes the creation of worlds to be followed first by their flood and then the destruction of heaven. Cf. the reference in ll. 22–4 of "A Nocturnall upon S. Lucies Day".

19–20 *O more . . . spheare:* i.e. She is more than the moon because that controls only the tides, and she can draw up whole seas of grief to drown him.

21 *in thine armes:* the place where he should be safe from danger and feel most alive.

26–7 *Since thou . . . death:* The lovers' breath is mingled as completely as their tears. Their souls are one (cf. "The Good-morrow", "A Valediction: forbidding mourning", "The Exstasie", and "The Canonization"); and the concluding image suggests the classical idea of the soul being breathed out in sighs (in both Greek and Latin the same word, *psyche* and *anima*, means either "breath" or "soul").

A VALEDICTION: FORBIDDING MOURNING

In this poem too Donne is taking leave of his mistress, and again employs
a metaphor of particular appeal for readers in his own day: that of a pair
of compasses in whose action he perceives a just analogy with the souls of
absent lovers (see Introduction, p. 8). Walton in his *Life* of Donne includes
a full text of the poem, which he says was given to Donne's wife when he
left her in 1611 to go with Sir Robert Drury to France. Helen Gardner
questions this on the strength of ll. 7–8—"not an argument to use to a wife,
who has no need to hide her grief at her husband's absence"—and sees the
poem as the address of a lover to his mistress (see footnote to ll. 11–12 of
"The Anniversarie", p. 40). At all events, this is another powerful evocation
of the experience of parting between a man and woman united by a bond of
more than usual intensity and identification with each other, whose relationship is at once passionate and rarefied. The compass image, with its two
final lines communicating a most satisfying sense of completion in reunion,
brilliantly achieves the familiar fusion in Donne of thought with feeling.
As Joan Bennett observes in *Five Metaphysical Poets*: "Such words as 'rome',
'leanes', 'hearkens' gather up emotion into the intellectual image. It seems,
as so often in Donne's poems, that one law is at work in all experience. The
same flame that lights the intellect warms the heart; mathematics and love
obey one principle. The binding of a circle and the union of lovers are
equivalent symbols of eternity and perfection."

There are slight variations in the text between the 1633 edition and the
manuscripts. The version used here follows Helen Gardner's preference in
her edition of *The Elegies and The Songs and Sonnets* (1965).

> As virtuous men passe mildly away,
>   And whisper to their soules, to goe,
> Whilst some of their sad friends doe say,
>   The breath goes now, and some say, no:
>
> 5 So let us melt, and make no noise,
>   No teare-floods, nor sigh-tempests move,
>   'Twere prophanation of our joyes
>   To tell the layetie our love.

Moving of th'earth brings harmes and feares,
10   Men reckon what it did and meant,
But trepidation of the spheares,
        Though greater farre, is innocent.

Dull sublunary lovers love
        (Whose soule is sense) cannot admit
15   Absence, because it doth remove
        Those things which elemented it.

But we by a love, so much refin'd,
        That our selves know not what it is,
Inter-assured of the mind,
20   Care lesse, eyes, lips, and hands to misse.

Our two soules therefore, which are one,
        Though I must goe, endure not yet
A breach, but an expansion,
        Like gold to ayery thinnesse beate.

25   If they be two, they are two so
        As stiffe twin compasses are two,
Thy soule the fixt foot, makes no show
        To move, but doth, if th'other doe.

And though it in the center sit,
30   Yet when the other far doth rome,
It leanes, and hearkens after it,
        And growes erect, as it comes home.

Such wilt thou be to mee, who must
        Like th'other foot, obliquely runne;
35   Thy firmnes makes my circle just,
        And makes me end, where I begunne.

---

6 *No teare-floods . . . move:* As in "A Valediction: of Weeping", the imagery of floods and tempests is appropriate to a journey overseas.

8 *the layetie:* This description of the everyday world suggests that their love is an activity essentially akin to religious experience (cf. "The Canonization" and especially "The Relique").

9–12 *Moving . . . innocent:* i.e. Earthquakes harm and alarm, causing men to reckon the damage and speculate on the portent, but the movement of the spheres, though far greater, does no harm and portends no ill. Donne refers to a belief in Ptolemaic astronomy about the movement of the earth's axis in relation to the sun. Helen Gardner explains that "The trepidation, or libration, of the ninth, the Crystalline, sphere, invented to account for the precession of the equinoxes, communicated itself to all the other spheres" (*The Metaphysical Poets*).

13-16 *Dull sublunary . . . elemented it:* i.e. In the regions below the moon (by contrast with the incorruptible heavens above them) ordinary lovers who experience their love through the senses cannot reconcile themselves to separation, because it removes the physical elements which composed that love.

17 *refin'd:* purified. This adjective continues the alchemical association of "elemented".

18 *That . . . is:* a common idea in Donne, that "refin'd" lovers cannot recognize the exact nature of their love. Cf. "Aire and Angels", l. 11, "The Exstasie", l. 30, "The Relique", l. 24, and "Negative Love", l. 15: "What we know not, our selves, can know".

19-20 *Inter-assured . . . misse:* i.e. Mutually assured of our more rarefied love (in "the mind"), we care less about the absence of the body.

21 *Our two . . . one:* Cf. the same idea of lovers' oneness in "The Good-morrow", ll. 14 and 20, "A Valediction: of Weeping", l. 26, "The Exstasie", ll. 35-6, and "The Canonization", l. 24 (and see also Introduction, p. 9).

24 *Like gold . . . beate:* This magnificent simile completes and crystallizes the alchemical references in "elemented" and "refin'd".

25-36 *If they . . . begunne:* The pair of compasses was a familiar contemporary emblem. Hall uses the image in *Epistles, The Second Volume*, 1608, Decade I, Epistle I, p. 6, to illustrate the action of faith and charity in the Christian heart, and Donne too employs it elsewhere, in his sermons and in the 'Obsequies to the Lord Harington', ll. 105-10. He develops the metaphor here with an incisive clarity which renders explanation largely unnecessary. At the end the beloved's fidelity ("firmnes") makes the soul of the wanderer, describing a circle which is constant and exact ("just") round the centre of his being, return home to its starting-point. Cf. Eliot's similar idea in *East Coker:*

> In my beginning is my end . . .
> Home is where one starts from . . .
> . . . In my end is my beginning.

AIRE AND ANGELS

DONNE draws liberally upon the doctrines of medieval Scholasticism for his ideas and images in this complex meditation which Helen Gardner has described as "a lecture in love's philosophy". She explains that the appearance of angels in visible form (a recurring idea in Vaughan too: see note to l. 2 of "The Retreate", p. 120) was accounted for "in scholastic theology by the theory that they made themselves 'bodies' of air condensed to clouds". This notion of the incarnation of pure spirit provides Donne with his central conceit, paralleled in the first stanza by the embodiment of his own soul in "limmes of flesh" and of love, child of that soul, materialized in the body of his beloved. Yet through the maritime metaphor in the following stanza he rejects her physical beauties as too excessive to be a fit vehicle for his love, which can no more dwell in things "scatt'ring bright"—"lip, eye, and brow", and every hair of her head—than in the shadowiness of a "lovely glorious nothing". He finally recognizes that it is only her love which can provide a satisfying "body" for his, as the air "contains" the angel; and this analogy defines the relative quality of men's and women's love in terms of the distinction between the purity of angels and that of the air they "wear". Donne's conclusion, based on a universally accepted theological assumption (to be found also in Shakespeare and many other contemporary writers, and outlined in the footnote, below, to ll. 26–8), has the effect of making this love poem seem more conventionally of his time than most of the others in this section, which boldly affirm an equal partnership between the sexes. Helen Gardner offers an extended and illuminating discussion of this apparent ambiguity in relation to the preceding lines, and of the whole poem, in *The Business of Criticism* (1959), pp. 62–75; and there is an acute appreciative analysis by A. J. Smith in *English* xiii, 1960, reprinted in *Twentieth-Century Views: John Donne*, ed. Helen Gardner (1962).

> Twice or thrice had I lov'd thee,
> Before I knew thy face or name;
> So in a voice, so in a shapeless flame,
> *Angells* affect us oft, and worship'd bee;
> 5   Still when, to where thou wert, I came,
> Some lovely glorious nothing I did see.

But since my soule, whose child love is,
Takes limmes of flesh, and else could nothing doe,
More subtile than the parent is,
10 Love must not be, but take a body too,
    And therefore what thou wert, and who,
      I bid Love aske, and now
That it assume thy body, I allow,
And fixe it selfe in thy lip, eye, and brow.

15 Whilst thus to ballast love, I thought,
And so more steddily to have gone,
With wares which would sinke admiration,
I saw, I had loves pinnace overfraught,
    Ev'ry thy haire for love to worke upon
20 Is much too much, some fitter must be sought;
    For, nor in nothing, nor in things
Extreme, and scatt'ring bright, can love inhere;
    Then as an Angell, face, and wings
Of aire, not pure as it, yet pure doth weare,
25   So thy love may be my loves spheare;
      Just such disparitie
As is twixt Aire and Angells puritie,
'Twixt womens love, and mens will ever bee.

1–2 *Twice . . . name:* i.e. My loves in the past were no more than an anticipation of the present reality. Cf. the similar statement in ll. 6–7 of "The Good-morrow".

3 *a shapeless flame:* not a steady burning, but a sudden flare of visionary light.

5 *Still:* always. **6** *Some lovely glorious nothing:* It was a Neo-Platonic commonplace, also expressed in Donne's "Negative Love", that the lover is constantly seeking some impalpable divinity beyond that enshrined in any particular body.

7–10 *But since . . . a body too:* i.e. The soul assumes a body; and since Love, its child, cannot exceed the parent in subtlety, it too cannot exist on earth except by taking a body.

11–14 *And therefore . . . brow:* i.e. Love is asked to identify its object, and allowed to find and fix its form in her.

15–18 *Whilst thus . . . overfraught:* i.e. While I thought to ballast love, in order to keep on a steadier course, with your physical perfections, I saw that I had overloaded my light craft. As Helen Gardner says, "wonder or admiration, which should be the beginning of knowledge, sinks beneath too much to admire and is destroyed".

22 *inhere:* Helen Gardner points out the theological connotation here. "The word 'assume' is common for the taking of flesh by the Son; but the word 'inhere' expresses another kind of relation, the relation of spirit to spirit" (*The Business of Criticism*, p. 67).

23–4 *Then as an Angell . . . weare:* i.e. Then as an angel, whose material form composed of air cannot, as a terrestrial substance, be as pure as its own celestial essence, but is nevertheless clothed in the purest of the four elements . . .

25 *So . . . spheare:* i.e. In the same way your love may be the sphere which mine can inhabit and govern. The Scholastic doctrine of the heavenly spheres, each ruled by an intelligence, originated in Aquinas, and is also employed by Donne in "The Exstasie", ll. 51–2.

26–8 *Just such . . . bee:* Because woman's place in the "great chain of being" of the medieval world-picture, inherited by Donne and his contemporaries, is lower than man's, so her love must necessarily be less ethereal than his. Speaking of the consequent "universal assumption of the superiority of all things masculine", Helen Gardner sees the lover in this poem as "the active, or masculine, principle seeking a proper passive complement . . . soul seeking a body, that is, form seeking matter to inform" (*The Elegies and The Songs and Sonnets*, Commentary, p. 205).

THE EXSTASIE

PROBABLY the most widely discussed of all Donne's poems, "The Exstasie" again explores his preoccupation in "Aire and Angels" with the relation between body and soul in love. It is also his subtlest and most profound metaphysical elaboration of the Neo-Platonic concept, introduced in "The Good-morrow", the two "Valedictions" included in this volume, and "The Canonization", of that oneness of being achieved by "pure" lovers. Coleridge declared of this poem: "I should never find fault with metaphysical poems, were they all like this, or but half as excellent". The central experience is of that "ecstasy" described by many Christian mystics, and elsewhere by Donne himself as "a departing, and secession, and suspension

of the soul" (*Letters*, p. 11): its liberation from the body and resulting state
of intense and clarified perception unhampered by reason or the senses. Yet
Donne also affirms, more explicitly and urgently than in any of his other
love poems, the interdependence of soul and body: that "soule into the
soule may flow,/Though it to body first repaire", and that the most rarefied
love is finally ineffective if it is not expressed through the medium of the
senses. The lovers' liberated souls, fused to form a single, more percipient
soul, cannot remain indefinitely suspended in an ecstatic trance of ideal
contemplation. Ultimately they must return, with the discovery they have
made of the true nature of their love which sets them apart from and above
the everyday world, to temporal reality and the bodies to which, as the
means of bringing their souls together, they owe gratitude. The image of
the body as love's "booke", the visible manifestation to ordinary men of the
soul's mysteries which have been vouchsafed to these lovers, carries the
sense of a divine revelation and gives, as in "The Canonization" and "The
Relique", and in the reference to "the layetie" in l. 8 of "A Valediction:
forbidding mourning", a religious association and significance to their
love.

> Where, like a pillow on a bed,
>   A Pregnant banke swel'd up, to rest
> The violets reclining head,
>   Sat we two, one anothers best;
>
> 5 Our hands were firmely cimented
>   With a fast balme, which thence did spring,
> Our eye-beames twisted, and did thred
>   Our eyes, upon one double string;
>
> So to'entergraft our hands, as yet
> 10   Was all our meanes to make us one,
> And pictures on our eyes to get
>   Was all our propagation.
>
> As 'twixt two equal Armies, Fate
>   Suspends uncertaine victorie,
> 15 Our soules, (which to advance their state,
>   Were gone out,) hung 'twixt her, and mee.
>
> And whil'st our soules negotiate there,
>   Wee like sepulchrall statues lay;

All day, the same our postures were,
20   And wee said nothing, all the day.

If any, so by love refin'd,
    That he soules language understood,
And by good love were grown all minde,
    Within convenient distance stood,

25 He (though he knew not which soule spake,
    Because both meant, both spake the same)
Might thence a new concoction take,
    And part farre purer then he came.

This Extasie doth unperplex
30   (We said) and tell us what we love,
Wee see by this, it was not sexe,
    Wee see, we saw not what did move:

But as all severall soules containe
    Mixture of things, they know not what,
35 Love, these mixt soules, doth mixe againe,
    And makes both one, each this and that.

A single violet transplant,
    The strength, the colour, and the size,
(All which before was poore, and scant,)
40   Redoubles still, and multiplies.

When love, with one another so
    Interinanimates two soules,
That abler soule, which thence doth flow,
    Defects of lonelinesse controules.

45 Wee then, who are this new soule, know,
    Of what we are compos'd, and made,
For, th'Atomies of which we grow,
    Are soules, whom no change can invade.

But O alas, so long, so farre
50   Our bodies why doe wee forbeare?
They'are ours, though they'are not wee, Wee are
    Th'intelligences, they the spheare.

We owe them thankes, because they thus,
  Did us, to us, at first convay,
55 Yeelded their forces, sense, to us,
  Nor are drosse to us, but allay.

On man heavens influence workes not so,
  But that it first imprints the ayre,
Soe soule into the soule may flow,
60   Though it to body first repaire.

As our blood labours to beget
  Spirits, as like soules as it can,
Because such fingers need to knit
  That subtile knot, which makes us man:

65 So must pure lovers soules descend
  T'affections, and to faculties,
That sense may reach and apprehend,
  Else a great Prince in prison lies.

To'our bodies turne wee then, that so
70   Weake men on love reveal'd may looke;
Loves mysteries in soules doe grow,
  But yet the body is his booke.

And if some lover, such as wee,
  Have heard this dialogue of one,
75 Let him still marke us, he shall see
  Small change, when we'are to bodies gone.

6 *a fast balme:* a warm moisture, "fast" perhaps in the double sense of "fastening" and "steadfast".

7–8 *Our eye-beames . . . string:* There was debate in Donne's time about the physical nature of sight: i.e. whether beams from the eye strike the object it sees, or beams from the object imprint its image on the eye. Donne's bold conceit communicates a vivid sense of the lovers' intimacy in the intermingling of their gaze.

9–10 *So to'entergraft . . . one:* i.e. Holding hands, like mingling glances, was so far our only means of physical or spiritual union.

11–12 *And pictures . . . propagation:* i.e. All we created between us was the reflection of each in the eyes of the other (a favourite image with Donne: see "The Good-morrow", ll. 15-16, "A Valediction: of Weeping", and "The Canonization", ll. 41-2). Helen Gardner explains that "The small image of oneself reflected in the pupils of another person was called a 'baby', from a pun on *pupilla*. For lovers thus to 'look babies' was a common idiom" (*The Elegies and The Songs and Sonnets*, Commentary, p. 184).

13-16 *As 'twixt . . . and mee:* i.e. Our souls, hanging in the air between our bodies which they have left, are like two opposing armies which have met "to advance their state": improve their dominant position, in the military sense, and perhaps also, as in one *OED* definition of "state", to put forward and settle "the point in question or debate between contending parties" (cf. "negotiate", l. 17). They are now engaged in a combat which is motionless because (being "equal") they can neither go forward nor withdraw.

17 *negotiate:* parley.

21-3 *so by love . . . all minde:* Cf. "A Valediction: forbidding mourning", ll. 17-19.

27 *a new concoction:* a continuation of the alchemical metaphor (l. 21) of metals and minerals refined by heat to a state of purity. The listener who could understand the conversation of souls might be thus reconstituted and go away ("part") further purified by overhearing theirs.

29-30 *This Extasie . . . love:* i.e. This separation of soul from body removes previous perplexities and reveals the real source of our love. See footnote to l. 18, "A Valediction: forbidding mourning".

31-2 *Wee see . . . move:* i.e. We see that it was not sexual attraction or desire; in this new clarity of perception we see that we did not understand before what moved us to love one another. This is the first recorded example, with l. 16 of "The Primrose", of the word "sex" used in its modern sense.

33-4 *But as . . . things:* Souls were regarded as being intermediate between the spiritual and the physical worlds, with a nature compounded of both, as otherwise they could not animate bodies; *they know not what:* i.e. we are as uncertain about the real composition of our souls as about that of our love. See footnote to ll. 29-30 above.

35-6 *Love . . . that:* i.e. The individual souls of the lovers, already mixed within themselves ("each this and that"), are further "re-mixed" by love's alchemy (cf. the central metaphor of "A Nocturnall upon S. Lucies Day") into the single, "abler" soul of l. 43.

37-40 *A single violet . . . multiplies:* Donne's analogy of the transplantation of flowers, harking back to the horticultural terms "entergraft" (l. 9) and "propagation" (l. 12), is taken from a popular idea of the period. He employs a similar metaphor in his Funeral Sermon on Lady Danvers (*Sermons,* viii, 87). Helen Gardner believes the choice here of the violet was "because it is a flower that exists in a single and a double form, and so provides an analogy with the creation of a new soul" (*The Elegies and The Songs and Sonnets,* p. 262).

44 *Defects . . . controules:* i.e. perfects whatever is faulty in each soul in its separate state.

45-8 *Wee then . . . invade:* i.e. This new soul, which has a complete understanding of its own nature, recognizes that, being equally mixed, it is beyond mutability or decay (see footnote to "The Good-morrow", ll 19-21)

50-1 *Our bodies . . . not wee:* i.e. Why do we abstain from, or deny, our bodies?—which belong to us although they are not our essence, which is the soul.

51-2 *Wee are . . . spheare:* See "Aire and Angels", l. 25 and footnote.

53-4 *they thus . . . convay:* i.e. through the clasped hands and commingled glances of ll. 5-8 they first brought us together.

55-6 *Yeelded . . . allay:* i.e. yielded up their faculties of the senses to us in order that our souls might perceive, and thus are not to be despised as worthless ("drosse") but regarded as the alloy which, as the inferior metal mixed with one of greater worth, is as necessary to it as the body is to the soul. This echoes the metaphor of ll. 27-8.

57-60 *On man . . . repaire:* Donne's analogy is drawn from the common belief that the stars influence man through the medium of the air. Thus the workings of "heavens influence" through material means parallels that of two souls fusing through a physical intermediary.

61-7 *As our blood . . . apprehend:* Burton in *The Anatomy of Melancholy* says that from the blood "*Spirits* are first begotten in the heart . . . a common tye or *medium* betwixt the body and the soul". Donne uses this idea again in *Sermons,* ii, 261-2: "In the constitution of a natural man, the body is not the man, nor the soul is not the man, but the union of these two makes up the man; the spirits in a man which are the thin and active part of the blood . . . doe the office, to unite and apply the faculties of the soul to the organs of the body, and so there is a man." The action of the blood, in striving to unite the physical and the intellectual in man, is here compared to that of the soul returning to the affections and faculties of the senses as its medium of communication.

63 *need:* are necessary.

68 *Else . . . lies:* The climactic affirmation of the interdependence of body and soul, expressed through one of Donne's favourite images (cf. "The

Sunne Rising", l. 21, and "The Anniversarie", l. 14). Here he means that if
the soul does not fulfil its function of informing and governing the body it is
like a powerful and sovereign ruler captive in his own kingdom. "Donne
is contrasting the Platonic view of the soul imprisoned in the flesh with the
Aristotelian conception of the union of the soul and body in man. A prince
is no prince if he does not rule his kingdom and a kingdom without a prince
is a chaos. Prince and kingdom need each other and are indeed inconceivable
without each other" (Helen Gardner, *The Elegies and The Songs and Sonnets*,
p. 265).

74 *this dialogue of one:* of our single, united soul.

75-6 *he shall see . . . bodies gone:* i.e. Because the knowledge of love's
mysteries, which live in the soul, will persist in the minds of "pure" lovers,
the listener will see little difference between their spiritual reality and their
physical manifestation when we have returned to our bodies.

A NOCTURNALL UPON S. LUCIES DAY, BEING
THE SHORTEST DAY

GRIERSON couples this magnificent and deeply moving elegiac poem with
"The Extasie", as one which "only Donne could have written . . . with the
same intensity of feeling, and in the same abstract, dialectical, erudite
strain" (*The Poems of John Donne*, 1912). Here Donne's theme is death, both
of the body (Grierson suggests that it was inspired by a serious illness of the
Countess of Bedford in 1612; but others have associated it with that of his
wife in 1611 or with her death in 1617) and of the spirit in the total desola-
tion of despair. St. Lucy's Day, the 13th of December, was regarded as the
shortest day of the year; and Donne equates the spiritual state in the microcosm, the lover bereft of his beloved, with that of the macrocosm in that
midwinter season which Eliot calls "the dark time of the year". Drawing
upon alchemy for his central metaphor, Donne explores the great antithesis
of All and Nothing which is the concern of so many of his sermons and
Essays in Divinity, and probes down to the very roots of the spiritual nothingness caused here by the death of his mistress. The art of alchemy was traditionally associated with the resurrection of the body, but Donne employs
its images to suggest the opposite—an absolute of annihilation. Through his
loss he has become both the "epitaph" and epitome of "every dead thing"
in nature, "the grave/Of all, that's nothing". The earth will be resurrected
from its deadness next spring, but there can be no corresponding rebirth

in the profound gloom of his spirit: "I am None; nor will my Sunne renew".
Unlike the temporary absences in the "Valedictions", or even his feelings
in poems like "The Canonization", "The Relique" and "The Anniversarie"
about the experience of lovers in death, this separation strikes a note of
sombre finality; and the dark, brooding mood of Donne's meditation is
exactly echoed in the sound-patterns and measured gravity of the metre.

'Tis the yeares midnight, and it is the dayes,
Lucies, who scarce seaven houres herself unmaskes,
   The Sunne is spent, and now his flasks
    Send forth light squibs, no constant rayes;
5   The world's whole sap is sunke:
The generall balme th'hydroptique earth hath drunk,
Whither, as to the beds-feet, life is shrunke,
Dead and enterr'd; yet all these seeme to laugh,
Compar'd with mee, who am their Epitaph.

10 Study me then, you who shall lovers bee
At the next world, that is, at the next Spring:
   For I am every dead thing,
    In whom love wrought new Alchimie.
    For his art did expresse
15 A quintessence even from nothingnesse,
From dull privations, and leane emptinesse:
He ruin'd mee, and I am re-begot
Of absence, darknesse, death; things which are not.

All others, from all things, draw all that's good,
20 Life, soule, forme, spirit, whence they beeing have;
   I, by loves limbecke, am the grave
    Of all, that's nothing. Oft a flood
    Have wee two wept, and so
Drownd the whole world, us two; oft did we grow
25 To be two Chaosses, when we did show
Care to ought else; and often absences
Withdrew our soules, and made us carcasses.

But I am by her death, (which word wrongs her)
Of the first nothing, the Elixer grown;

30 Were I a man, that I were one,
   I needs must know; I should preferre,
      If I were any beast,
   Some ends, some means; Yea plants, yea stones detest,
   And love; All, all some properties invest;
35 If I an ordinary nothing were,
   As shadow, a light, and body must be here.

   But I am None; nor will my Sunne renew.
   You lovers, for whose sake, the lesser Sunne
      At this time to the Goat is runne
40 To fetch new lust, and give it you,
      Enjoy your summer all;
   Since shee enjoyes her long nights festivall,
   Let mee prepare towards her, and let mee call
   This houre her Vigill, and her Eve, since this
45 Both the yeares, and the dayes deep midnight is.

3 *flasks:* the stars. These were believed to store up light from the sun.

6 *The generall balme . . . drunk:* In Paracelsian philosophy this "balm" was an organic substance which preserved the life in all things. The already sodden winter earth has drunk up even this, like a man swollen with dropsy ("hydroptique") who still experiences great thirst.

7 *Whither . . . shrunke:* The life of nature has shrunk into the earth as a dying man does to the foot of the bed. Helen Gardner quotes in illustration from *The Book of the Presages of the divine Hippocrates*, 1597: "Likewise when the sicke turneth, wrings and tosseth up and downe often times with starting either in sleepe or waking, and making the beds feet where the head should be, casting himself downe, not knowing what he doth, is an evill signe."

12-18 *For I am . . . which are not:* i.e. Love, in robbing me of her, is like an alchemist who "expresses" (presses out, extracts) the pure and concentrated essence even from the nothingness of privation and emptiness caused by her death. In the same way as the alchemist abstracts the form from metals he wishes to reconstitute as gold, love has "ruined" my being in order to produce from it a new form which is the quintessence of "every dead thing", of "absence, darknesse, death"—all that spells total negation.

21 *limbecke:* the vessel used by the alchemist for distillation.

22-4 *Oft a flood . . . the whole world:* Cf. "A Valediction: of Weeping", ll. 14-18.

24–7 *oft did we grow . . . carcasses:* i.e. Often neglect of each other for other concerns wrought a division of our one united being into two separate "chaoses"; and often physical separation, in withdrawing our souls, made us dead bodies. (These three kinds of grief known to their *living* love lead to the climax of the final and absolute separation of the next two lines.)

29 *Of the first nothing . . . grown:* i.e. Through her death (even the word does her injury) I have become the quintessence of that primal nothingness which preceded creation (of which Donne wrote, in *Essays in Divinity*, "being no creature, is more incomprehensible than all the rest").

30–7 *Were I a man . . . renew:* i.e. If I were a man, I should know it by means of my reason, If I were a beast, I should be able to choose some ends and means; plants, in so far as they can select and reject their food, can "detest" and "love", and so even can stones (cf. Donne's Christmas Sermon of 1629, *Sermons*, ix, 147: "We are not sure that stones have not life; stones may have life"). All possess *some* properties; even if I were an "ordinary" nothing like a shadow, that must be caused by light and form. But I am the quintessence of Nothingness; nor will the light of my life, and she who was its cause, be renewed.

38–40 *the lesser Sunne . . . new lust:* i.e. the sun which is lesser than his dead mistress, and which now enters the zodiacal sign of Capricorn, the Goat, symbol of lust.

42–5 *Since . . . midnight is:* The saint whose vigil he keeps is simultaneously Lucy and his dead love; to whom, leaving the renewing spring and coming summer to lesser lovers, he turns back in this time of darkness and deadness.

THE CANONIZATION

COLERIDGE called this "one of [his] favourite poems". Here Donne rejects worldly arguments against love, which in its other-worldliness is compared with religious experience and leads eventually to the lovers' canonization as saints. With an aggressive abruptness which recalls the opening of "The Sunne Rising" he adjures the world to occupy itself with its accustomed pursuits and let him alone to his love, which may seem to it insignificant and can in no way affect or damage its material affairs. In his subtle analysis of the nature of love which follows, all contradictions and apparent duality are resolved in the image of the self-immolation of the Phoenix. This miraculous fusion of two souls into a perfect whole is the "oneness" also evoked by ll. 14 and 20 of "The Good-morrow", in the two "Valedictions", and above all in "The Exstasie". The final concept of love's all-sufficiency (ll. 40–4), through which lovers encompass within their private experience that of the whole world, echoes the thought in the last stanza of "The Sunne Rising". The testy irascibility and rapid, staccato movement of the first verse gradually change in tone and tempo as the poem progresses; and the word "love", which concludes the first and last lines of each stanza and is the basic rhyming-word throughout, is skilfully reiterated.

    For Godsake hold your tongue, and let me love,
      Or chide my palsie, or my gout,
    My five gray haires, or ruin'd fortune flout,
      With wealth your state, your minde with Arts improve,
5   Take you a course, get you a place,
      Observe his honour, or his grace,
    Or the Kings reall, or his stamped face
      Contemplate, what you will, approve,
      So you will let me love.

10 Alas, alas, who's injur'd by my love?
      What merchants ships have my sighs drown'd?
    Who saies my teares have overflow'd his ground?
      When did my colds a forward spring remove?
      When did the heats which my veines fill
15   Adde one man to the plaguie Bill?
    Soldiers finde warres, and Lawyers finde out still
      Litigious men, which quarrels move,
      Though she and I do love.

    Call us what you will, wee are made such by love;
20   Call her one, mee another flye,
    We'are Tapers too, and at our owne cost die,
      And wee in us finde the'Eagle and the Dove.
      The Phoenix ridle hath more wit
      By us, we two being one, are it,
25 So to one neutrall thing both sexes fit.
      Wee dye and rise the same, and prove
      Mysterious by this love.

Wee can dye by it, if not live by love,
  And if unfit for tombes and hearse
30 Our legend bee, it will be fit for verse;
    And if no peece of Chronicle wee prove,
      We'll build in sonnets pretty roomes;
      As well a well wrought urne becomes
    The greatest ashes, as halfe-acre tombes,
35   And by these hymnes, all shall approve
      Us *Canoniz'd* for Love:

And thus invoke us; You whom reverend love
  Made one anothers hermitage;
You, to whom love was peace, that now is rage;
40 Who did the whole worlds soule extract, and drove
    Into the glasses of your eyes
    (So made such mirrors, and such spies,
  That they did all to you epitomize,)
  Countries, Townes, Courts: Beg from above
45 A patterne of your love!

2 *Or chide:* either chide.

3 *ruin'd fortune:* Possibly a reference to the ruin of Donne's secular career through his secret marriage in 1601 to Ann More, niece of his employer, Sir Thomas Egerton.

4 *state:* estate: property, possessions.

5 *Take you a course:* follow a career.

5–8 *get you a place . . . Contemplate:* i.e. get yourself a position of importance by cultivating a lord or a bishop, attend the King at Court, or amass money (the coinage with his face stamped on it). As in "The Sunne Rising", l. 7, the last reference dates composition after 1603.

8 *what you will, approve:* try what you will.

9 *So:* if only.

12 *Who saies . . . ground?:* This would be a cause for complaint with the quarrelsome, "litigious" men of l. 17.

13 *When . . . remove:* i.e. When did my coldness in love retard the spring? (thus injuring the farmers).

15 *Adde . . . Bill?:* add one name to the weekly printed bills of mortality from the plague.

17 *which quarrels move:* who stir up disputes.

20–1 *Call her . . . die:* The image of flies suggests their insignificance in the world's eyes. But the lovers are also simultaneously moths and tapers: i.e. as the first they circle the tapers' flame and are thus destroyed by each other, as the second they burn and are self-consumed.

22 *the Eagle and the Dove:* common contemporary symbols of strength and gentleness (cf. Crashaw's poem to St. Teresa: "By all the Eagle in thee, all the Dove").

23–7 *The Phoenix ridle . . . love:* i.e. The mystery of the fabulous bird which burned itself to death and rose renewed from its ashes makes more sense because of us, for in "two being one" (the Phoenix was sexless and self-propagating) we exemplify it. Thus in this single being, with sex neutralized, we die (in the act of love) and are regenerated in the same form from the fire of passion.

29 *hearse:* Memorial inscriptions were hung on hearses.

31 *And if . . . prove:* i.e. And if the legend of our love will not prove a fit subject for history.

32 *sonnets pretty roomes:* A pun, on the verses of love-songs (sonnets) and the Italian for "room" (*stanza*).

35 *approve:* confirm.

37–45 *And thus invoke . . . love!:* i.e. All shall request the prayers of the lovers canonized as saints, who are asked to beg from heaven a pattern of their love for men below to follow.

39 *to whom . . . rage:* i.e. who found in each other the fulfilment which transcends the customary conflicts of love (cf. *Sermons*, i, 237: "To desire without fruition, is a rage.").

40 *extract:* distil. The 1633 edition of Donne's poems (the version which appears in many anthologies) gives the verb "contract". But Helen Gardner, in her 1965 editing of *The Elegies and The Songs and Sonnets*, prefers "extract", the reading in all the manuscripts, as being more consistent with the alchemical metaphor, the pun on "glasses", and the verb "drove". She interprets the meaning of ll. 40–2 thus: "The 'soul' of the world is extracted and driven into their eyes as an alchemist makes an extract by sublimation and distillation, driving it through the pipes of the still into the 'glasses', or vessels, in which it is stored. These 'glasses' then become mirrors."

41–2 *Into the glasses . . . mirrors:* Cf. the similar "reflection"-images in "A Valediction: of Weeping" and ll. 15–16 of "The Good-morrow".

42–4 *and such spies . . . Courts:* i.e. "spies" on all experience, so that they epitomize to you the whole sum of human activity everywhere.

THE RELIQUE

THIS variation on the theme of dead lovers worshipped as saints also strongly
recalls the ideas and imagery of Donne's poem "The Funerall". Grierson's
suggestion that it was addressed to Mrs. Magdalen Herbert, Donne's close
friend and benefactor for many years, is supported by the allusion to her
Christian name in l. 17 (but questioned by Helen Gardner). As in many of
Donne's poems, both secular and divine, love, death and religion are in
separable. His tone is ironic as he contemplates the imagined folly of future
generations in idolatrously venerating him and his lady after mistaking the
bracelet of hair, symbol of a human attachment, for one of religious power.
Yet the development of the poem's conceits and its play on the nature of
"miracles" makes the mysteries of religion and those of love by implication
synonymous. For all the urbanity of its treatment and the sardonic metaphysical wit, Donne is presenting a profoundly serious conception of the
natural miracle of human love, which aspires to defy the grave itself and
equals any miraculous supernatural manifestation which men may seek.

When my grave is broke up againe
Some second guest to entertaine,
(For graves have learn'd that woman-head
To be to more than one a Bed)
5   And he that digs it, spies
A bracelet of bright haire about the bone,
Will he not let'us alone,
And thinke that there a loving couple lies,
Who thought that this device might be some way
10   To make their soules, at the last busie day,
Meet at this grave, and make a little stay?

If this fall in a time, or land,
Where mis-devotion doth command,
Then, he that digges us up, will bring
15   Us, to the Bishop, and the King,
To make us Reliques; then
Thou shalt be a Mary Magdalen, and I

A something else thereby;
All women shall adore us, and some men;
20 And since at such time, miracles are sought,
I would have that age by this paper taught
What miracles wee harmelesse lovers wrought.

First, we lov'd well and faithfully,
Yet knew not what wee lov'd, nor why,
25   Difference of sex no more wee knew,
Than our Guardian Angells doe;
Comming and going, wee
Perchance might kisse, but not between those meales;
Our hands ne'er toucht the seales,
30 Which nature, injur'd by late law, sets free:
These miracles wee did; but now alas,
All measure, and all language, I should passe,
Should I tell what a miracle shee was.

1-2 *When my grave . . . entertaine:* It was common practice in the crowded burial grounds of Donne's time to dig up old graves to make room for new occupants.

3-4 *(For . . . Bed):* i.e. For graves have learned that trick of feminine nature (note the echo of "maidenhead") of being a bed for more than one person.

6 *A bracelet . . . bone:* One of Donne's magical lines. Eliot notes "the most powerful effect . . . produced by the sudden contrast of associations"— the sense of triumphant continuing life in the "bright haire" with the deadness of the bone.

7 *Will . . . alone:* Cf. the similar plea by the lover in stanza 1 of "The Canonization" to be "let alone".

10 *the last busie day:* of resurrection and Judgment.

12-13 *If this . . . command:* i.e. if my disinterment should happen at a time or in a country in which idolatrous religion is practised.

15 *to the Bishop, and the King:* to be recognized and translated as relics.

17-18 *Thou . . . thereby:* i.e. The superstitious will identify the woman with this saint by the "bright haire" with which she is traditionally represented in art; and because of this they will take the man to be one of her lovers wearing her token.

19 *All women . . . men:* a dry distinction between the sexes which ironically suggests both the greater gullibility of women in adoring religious relics and their more serious interest in the subject of love.

20 *And since . . . sought:* i.e. And since the credulous will look for miracles at the time our relics are authenticated.

21 *this paper:* this poem.

22 *harmelesse:* the epithet underlines the central theme—that miracles need not be sought solely in supernatural manifestations but are perfectly possible within ordinary human experience, as enumerated in the third stanza.

24 *what wee lov'd:* what in each other. See footnote to l. 18 of "A Valediction: forbidding mourning", p. 00.

25–6 *Difference . . . doe:* The miracle of platonic love (cf. also "The Canonization", l. 25).

27–8 *Comming . . . meales:* i.e. On visits we might exchange the customary formal kisses of greeting and parting, but not between those "meals", in the sense of the kisses as food of their love.

29–30 *Our hands . . . free:* i.e. We never attempted to enjoy the physical union urged by nature but restrained by more recent human law.

31 *These . . . did:* Donne sees as miraculous the fact that a man and woman who have "lov'd well and faithfully" should also have obeyed the rules of conventional moral conduct; *alas:* The word, taken with the use of the past tense in the last line, suggests grief for a love already dead as he writes.

THE ANNIVERSARIE

As in the last stanza of "The Sunne Rising", Donne likens his lovers to Princes, supreme rulers through the power of their experience over all other forms of temporal life. The triumphant certitude of his faith in the permanence of his love and the safety it confers, and a deep sense of fulfilment, are vividly conveyed by the slow, measured cadences, swelling and coming to rest in the long line at the close of each stanza. "One feels," says Grierson, "the quickening of the brain, the vision extending its range, the passion gathering sweep with the expanding rhythms . . . purified and enriched by being brought into harmony with his whole nature, spiritual as well as physical. . . . In love, says Pascal, the body disappears from sight in the intellectual and spiritual passion which it has kindled. That is what happens in 'The Anniversarie'" (Introduction to his edition of Donne's *Poems*, 1912).

All Kings, and all their favorites,
   All glory of honors, beauties, wits,
The Sun it selfe, which makes times, as they passe,
Is elder by a yeare, now, than it was
5 When thou and I first one another saw:
All other things, to their destruction draw,
   Only our love hath no decay;
This, no to morrow hath, nor yesterday,
Running it never runs from us away,
10 But truly keepes his first, last, everlasting day.

Two graves must hide thine and my corse,
   If one might, death were no divorce.
Alas, as well as other Princes, wee,
(Who Prince enough in one another bee,)
15 Must leave at last in death, these eyes, and eares,
Oft fed with true oathes, and with sweet salt teares;
   But soules where nothing dwells but love
(All other thoughts being inmates) then shall prove
This, or a love increased there above,
20 When bodies to their graves, soules from their graves remove.

And then wee shall be throughly blest,
   But wee no more, than all the rest;
Here upon earth, we'are Kings, and none but wee
Can be such Kings, nor of such subjects bee.
25 Who is so safe as wee? where none can doe
Treason to us, except one of us two.
   True and false feares let us refraine,
Let us love nobly, and live, and adde againe
Yeares and yeares unto yeares, till we attaine
30 To write threescore: this is the second of our raigne.

1–2 *All Kings . . . wits:* Helen Gardner notes the same scorn for the Court of James, from which Donne was an exile, as in "The Sunne Rising" and the first verse of "The Canonization".

3 *The Sun . . . passe:* i.e. which creates the hours, days, months, etc. (cf. "The Sunne Rising", l. 10; also *The second Anniversary*, l. 23: "Before the Sunne, which fram'd the daies, was fram'd"). All the subjects of the first two lines, as well as the sun itself, maker of time, are a year older since he and she met.

8–10 *This . . . day:* i.e. The timelessness of love defies the natural laws of decay and death (cf. "The Sunne Rising", ll. 9–10).

11–12 *Two graves . . . divorce:* The lovers are unmarried, or they would be buried together (as Donne, in his epitaph for her grave, hoped to be buried with his wife).

14 (*Who Prince . . . bed,*): i.e. who rule in each other as powerfully as worldly princes. This was a favourite image with Donne (cf. "The Sunne Rising", l. 21, and "The Exstasie", l. 68).

17 *dwells:* lives permanently.

18 *inmates:* mere lodgers or visitors, not inhabitants.

18–20 *then shall prove . . . remove:* i.e. then shall experience this love to the full, or one even greater in heaven, when bodies go to their graves in earth and souls depart from theirs of the body.

21 *throughly:* thoroughly.

22 *But . . . rest:* i.e. All shall be equally blessed with perfect happiness in heaven (although as Grierson points out, Scholastic philosophy held that there all are not equally blessed but equally *content*).

23–6 *Here upon earth . . . two:* i.e. It is here on earth that we are greater than the rest, "Kings" through the power of our love: without rivals, for none can be such kings and such subjects as we are to each other, and none so safe where only each can betray the other.

27 *True and false:* real and imaginary.

28–30 *Let us . . . raigne:* The poem ends on a note of exultation, not in the prospect of a common felicity after death or even of "a love increased there above", but in the supremacy of their present "reign" on earth.

Sir Henry Wotton

ON HIS MISTRIS, THE *QUEEN* OF *BOHEMIA*

SIR HENRY WOTTON (1568–1639) was Donne's close friend. Wotton's death prevented his writing the biography he intended, and this was left to Walton, who had been employed to collect material for it. Donne too wrote a poem celebrating the occasion of these verses—the marriage in 1613 of Princess Elizabeth, daughter of James I, to Frederick, Elector Palatine.

> You meaner *Beauties* of the *Night*,
> That poorly satisfie our *Eies*
> More by your *number*, than your *light*,
> You *Common people* of the *Skies*;
> 5   What are you when the *Moon* shall rise?
>
> You curious Chanters of the Wood,
> That warble forth *Dame Natures* layes,
> Thinking your *Passions* understood
> By your weake *accents*; whats your praise
> 10   When *Philomell* her voyce shal raise?
>
> You *Violets*, that first appeare,
> By your *pure purpel mantels* knowne,
> Like the proud *Virgins* of the *yeare*,
> As if the *Spring* were all your own;
> 15   What are you when the *Rose is blowne*?
>
> So, when my *Mistris* shal be *seene*
> In *form* and *Beauty* of her *mind*,
> By *Vertue* first, then *Choyce* a Queen,
> Tell me, if *she* were not design'd
> 20   Th' *Eclypse* and *Glory* of her kind.

1–4 *You meaner* Beauties . . . Skies: the stars.
There are varying versions of this poem. This eclectic text is the one preferred by Helen Gardner.

Henry King

THE EXEQUY

HENRY KING, Bishop of Chichester, was another friend of Donne, who was ordained in 1615 by his father, then Bishop of London. In 1617, the year Donne's wife died, King married Anne Berkeley, who also died only seven years later. His elegy on her, with its controlled meditative structure intermittently punctuated by a poignant exclamation of personal grief and loss, is among the most moving in the language. T. S. Eliot has called it "one of the finest poems of the age (a poem which could not have been written in any other age)", and added that the work of King, with that of Marvell, is "sometimes nearer than any of the other authors" to the poetry of Donne. King's use of the octosyllabic couplet is flexible, and his rebellious rebuke to the earth which has claimed her (ll. 61–80) breaks in upon the orthodox Christian sentiments immediately preceding it with the colloquial directness of dramatic blank verse.

> Accept thou Shrine of my dead Saint,
> Insteed of Dirges this complaint;
> And for sweet flowres to crown thy hearse,
> Receive a strew of weeping verse
> 5 From thy griev'd friend, whom thou might'st see
> Quite melted into tears for thee.
>
> Dear loss! since thy untimely fate
> My task hath been to meditate
> On thee, on thee: thou art the book,
> 10 The library whereon I look

Though almost blind. For thee (lov'd clay)
I languish out, not live the day,
Using no other exercise
But what I practise with mine eyes:
15 By which wet glasses I find out
How lazily time creeps about
To one that mourns: this, onely this
My exercise and bus'ness is:
So I compute the weary houres
20 With sighs dissolved into showres.

　　Nor wonder if my time go thus
Backward and most preposterous;
Thou hast benighted me, thy set
This Eve of blackness did beget,
25 Who was't my day, (though overcast
Before thou had'st thy Noon-tide past)
And I remember must in tears,
Thou scarce had'st seen so many years
As Day tells houres. By thy cleer Sun
30 My life and fortune first did run;
But thou wilt never more appear
Folded within my Hemisphear,
Since both thy light and motion
Like a fled Star is fall'n and gon,
35 And twixt me and my soules dear wish
The earth now interposed is,
Which such a strange eclipse doth make
As ne're was read in Almanake.

　　I could allow thee for a time
40 To darken me and my sad Clime,
Were it a month, a year, or ten,
I would thy exile live till then;
And all that space my mirth adjourn,
So thou wouldst promise to return;
45 And putting off thy ashy shrowd
At length disperse this sorrows cloud.

But woe is me! the longest date
Too narrow is to calculate
These empty hopes: never shall I
50 Be so much blest as to descry
A glimpse of thee, till that day come
Which shall the earth to cinders doome,
And a fierce Feaver must calcine
The body of this world like thine,
55 (My little World!). That fit of fire
Once off, our bodies shall aspire
To our soules bliss: then we shall rise
And view our selves with cleerer eyes
In that calm Region, where no night
60 Can hide us from each others sight.

Mean time, thou hast her, earth: much good
May my harm do thee. Since it stood
With Heavens will I might not call
Her longer mine, I give thee all
65 My short-liv'd right and interest
In her, whom living I lov'd best:
With a most free and bounteous grief,
I give thee what I could not keep.
Be kind to her, and prethee look
70 Thou write into thy Dooms-day book
Each parcell of this Rarity
Which in thy Casket shrin'd doth ly:
See that thou make thy reck'ning streight,
And yield her back again by weight;
75 For thou must audit on thy trust
Each graine and atome of this dust,
As thou wilt answer *Him* that lent,
Not gave thee, my dear Monument.

So close the ground, and 'bout her shade
80 Black curtains draw, my *Bride* is laid.

Sleep on my *Love* in thy cold bed
Never to be disquieted!
My last good night! Thou wilt not wake
Till I thy fate shall overtake:
85 Till age, or grief, or sickness must
Marry my body to that dust
It so much loves; and fill the room
My heart keeps empty in thy Tomb.
Stay for me there; I will not faile
90 To meet thee in that hollow Vale.
And think not much of my delay;
I am already on the way,
And follow thee with all the speed
Desire can make, or sorrows breed.
95 Each minute is a short degree,
And ev'ry houre a step towards thee.
At night when I betake to rest,
Next morn I rise neerer my West
Of life, almost by eight houres saile,
100 Than when sleep breath'd his drowsie gale.

Thus from the Sun my Bottom stears,
And my dayes Compass downward bears:
Nor labour I to stemme the tide
Through which to *Thee* I swiftly glide.

105 'Tis true, with shame and grief I yield,
Thou like the *Vann* first took'st the field,
And gotten hast the victory
In thus adventuring to dy
Before me, whose more years might crave
110 A just precedence in the grave.
But heark! My pulse like a soft Drum
Beats my approch, tells *Thee* I come;
And slow howere my marches be,
I shall at last sit down by *Thee*.

115   The thought of this bids me go on,
        And wait my dissolution
        With hope and comfort. *Dear* (forgive
        The crime) I am content to live
        Divided, with but half a heart,
120   Till we shall meet and never part.

4 *a strew:* a noun derived from the verb "to strew" (scatter).
11 *almost blind:* with weeping.
23 *thy set:* the setting of your sun.
31–8 *But thou . . . Almanake:* His bereavement is communicated through images often used also by Donne, of hemisphere, falling star, and the sun's eclipse. "The earth" (l. 36) is a pun: earth's shadow between him and his sun causes an eclipse; and earth covers her body in the grave.
51–4 *that day . . . thine:* the day of Judgment.
55 (*My Little World!*): Cf. "The Good-morrow", l. 14.
71 *parcell:* part.
73–5 *See that . . . trust:* Cf. the similar "accountancy" imagery in Crashaw's "Upon the Death of a Gentleman", pp. 59–60).
78 *my dear Monument:* her body, the "Shrine" of l. 1.
79–80 *So close . . . laid:* The verb "laid", taken with reference to the curtains of a bed and the word "*Bride*", may also carry the suggestion of the bridal night as well as the obvious one of burial in the grave. Cf. Vaughan's reference to the bed as a "Curtain'd grave" in "The Morning-watch", p. 116, ll. 31–2.
92–104 *I am already . . . glide:* T. S. Eliot notes how this figure of a journey, expressing the writer's impatience to join his dead wife, affords a perfect illustration of "the extended comparison . . . the idea and the simile become one". It recalls Donne's geographical images of voyage and discovery in "The Good-morrow"; also cf. ll. 98–9 ("neerer my West/Of life") with l. 11 of "Hymne to God my God, in my sicknesse".
101 *Thus . . . stears:* his vessel steers away from the sun—i.e. towards death, as also in l. 102.
106 *the* Vann: vanguard of an army. The conceit of the voyage has changed to a military one.

Thomas Carew

TO MY INCONSTANT MISTRIS

GRIERSON calls Thomas Carew (1594/5–1640) "the poetic ornament" of the Court of Charles I, seeing in his poems and Vandyke's pictures its "artistic taste . . . vividly reflected, a dignified voluptuousness, an exquisite elegance". The theme of this poem had been used by the classical poets Catullus and Propertius. Its blend of ironical wit with passion is typically metaphysical, and the use in a love poem of the religious conceit of excommunication, apostasy and damnation recalls Donne's employment of erotic imagery in his divine poems (see ll. 9–14 of the Holy Sonnet "Batter my heart", p. 80).

When thou, poore excommunicate
   From all the joyes of love, shalt see
The full reward, and glorious fate,
   Which my strong faith shall purchase me,
5   Then curse thine owne inconstancie.

A fayrer hand than thine, shall cure
   That heart, which thy false oathes did wound;
And to my soule, a soule more pure
   Than thine, shall by Loves hand be bound,
10   And both with equall glory crown'd.

Then shalt thou weepe, entreat, complaine
   To Love, as I did once to thee;
When all thy teares shall be as vaine
   As mine were then, for thou shalt bee
15   Damn'd for thy false Apostasie.

MARIA WENTWORTH

Thomae *Comitis* Cleveland, *filia*
praemortua prima Virgineam animam exhalavit
An. Dom. 1632. AEt. suae 18

THE second daughter of Sir Thomas Wentworth, afterwards Earl of Cleveland, Maria died at the age of eighteen in January 1632/3, and was buried in St. George's Church at Toddington in Bedfordshire, where her tomb may still be seen inscribed with the first six stanzas of Carew's epitaph. She is depicted by the sculptor as a seated figure with a sewing-basket, which perhaps gave rise to the pious local tradition that she died from pricking her finger while sewing on a Sunday. Carew was a friend of her maternal uncle John Crofts, with whom he had been in the service of Lord Herbert of Cherbury. He later composed a "Hymeneall Song" for the marriage in 1638 of Maria's younger sister Anne, to whom Richard Lovelace dedicated his *Lucasta* in 1649. The two opening stanzas of the present poem repeat the idea of the fatal frailty of that "clayie tenement", the flesh, in being unable to contain the "flame" of the spirit, which Carew had already expressed in the second of his epitaphs on the Lady Mary Villiers. Cf. also Dryden, *Absalom and Achitophel*, 156–8:

> A fiery Soul, which working out its way,
> Fretted the Pigmy Body to decay:
> And o'r informed the Tenement of Clay.

The graceful lightness and almost Augustan elegance of the three-line rhyming stanzas suddenly concentrate into the impact of the brilliant conceit in the penultimate one: a flash of metaphysical wit at its most epigrammatically effective, by which in a sense the somewhat conventionally unremarkable sentiments of the whole epitaph are themselves "justifi'd".

> And here the precious dust is layd;
> Whose purely temper'd Clay was made
> So fine, that it the guest betray'd.
>
> Else the soule grew so fast within,
> 5 It broke the outward shell of sinne,
> And so was hatch'd a Cherubin.

In heigth, it soar'd to God above;
In depth, it did to knowledge move,
And spread in breadth to generall love.

10 Before, a pious duty shind
To Parents, courtesie behind,
On either side an equall mind,

Good to the Poore, to kindred deare,
To servants kind, to friendship cleare,
15 To nothing but her selfe, severe.

So though a Virgin, yet a Bride
To every Grace, she justifi'd
A chaste Poligamie, and dy'd.

Learne from hence (Reader) what small trust
20 We owe this world, where vertue must
Fraile as our flesh, crumble to dust.

3 *the guest:* the life it housed.
4–6 *Else . . . Cherubin:* Donne uses this conceit in "Of the Progresse of the Soule. The second Anniversary", ll. 183–4: ". . . This to thy Soule allow,/ Thinke thy shell broke, thinke thy Soule hatch'd but now". So also does Cleveland: "Hatch him whom Nature poach'd but Half a Man" ("To P. Rupert", l. 106).
14 *cleare:* pure, guileless, innocent.
15 *To nothing . . . severe:* Cf. Donne, "Of the Progresse of the Soule. The second Anniversary", l. 368: "For, only herself except, she pardon'd all".

William Habington

AGAINST THEM WHO LAY UNCHASTITY
TO THE SEX OF WOMEN

THIS spirited affirmation that beauty does not preclude chastity in woman is a rejoinder to the provocation of Donne's statement in "Goe, and catche a falling starre" that "No where/Lives a woman true and fair." There is also a challenge in l. 12 here to l. 24 of "The Sunne Rising" ("All wealth alchimie"). The poem is taken from *Castara* (1634), celebrating Habington's courtship and marriage the previous year to Lucy Herbert, daughter of Lord Powys.

> They meet but with unwholesome Springs,
> And Summers which infectious are:
> They heare but when the Meremaid sings,
> And only see the falling starre:
> 5   Who ever dare,
> Affirme no woman chaste and faire.
>
> Goe cure your feavers: and you'le say
> The Dog-dayes scorch not all the yeare:
> In Copper Mines no longer stay,
> 10 But travell to the West, and there
>   The right ones see:
> And grant all gold's not Alchimie.
>
> What mad man 'cause the glow-wormes flame
> Is cold, sweares there's no warmth in fire?
> 15 'Cause some make forfeit of their name,

And slave themselves to mans desire;
    Shall the sex free
From guilt, damn'd to the bondage be?

Nor grieve, *Castara*, though 'twere fraile,
20 Thy Vertue then would brighter shine,
When thy example should prevaile,
And every womans faith be thine,
    And were there none;
'Tis Majesty to rule alone.

---

3 *They heare . . . sings:* Cf. l. 5 of Donne's poem: "Goe, and catche a falling starre": "Teach me to hear mermaids singing"; as the next line refers to l. 1 of the same poem.

8 *Dog-dayes:* the hottest part of the summer.

10 *the West:* Cf. "The Sunne Rising", l. 17, where the West Indies is the place of the gold-mines.

Sir William Davenant

THE SOULDIER GOING TO THE FIELD

SIR WILLIAM DAVENANT (1606–68), successor to Jonson as Poet Laureate, was the author of poems, masques and plays and after the Restoration became a leading figure in the London theatre. He also had personal experience of action as a soldier, and draws on it here to elaborate the conceit of the interchange of hearts between lovers.

> Preserve thy sighs, unthrifty Girle!
>   To purifie the Ayre;
> Thy Teares to Thrid instead of Pearle,
>   On Bracelets of thy Hair.

> 5 The Trumpet makes the Eccho hoarse
>   And wakes the louder Drum;
> Expence of grief gains no remorse,
>   When sorrow should be dumb.

> For I must go where lazy Peace,
> 10   Will hide her drouzy head;
> And, for the sport of Kings, encrease
>   The number of the Dead.

> But first I'le chide thy cruel theft:
>   Can I in War delight,
> 15 Who being of my heart bereft,
>   Can have no heart to fight?

Thou knowst the Sacred Laws of old,
   Ordain'd a Thief should pay,
To quit him of his Theft, seavenfold
20   What he had stoln away.

Thy payment shall but double be;
   O then with speed resign
My own seduced Heart to me,
   Accompani'd with thine.

---

3 *Thrid:* thread.

7-8 *Expence . . . dumb:* i.e. Your expressions of grief arouse no pity in me at a time it should be silent.

17-20 *the Sacred Laws . . . stoln away :* See *Proverbs* vi, 30-1.

Edmund Waller

OF THE LAST VERSES IN THE BOOK

ONE of the leading Royalist gentlemen of his day, Edmund Waller (1606–87) was banished after his involvement in 1643 as the leader in a plot to seize London for Charles I, and, like Crashaw, spent some time in exile in Paris before his return to favour at the Restoration. This meditation on the human condition on the threshold of death was published in 1686, and its title refers to the divine poems which Waller had added to the previous edition of his *Poems* four years earlier, at the age of seventy-six. His theme, that the body's weakening and decay enable the strengthening of the spirit (ll. 3–6) and that time and age bring it fresh illumination (ll. 13–14), recalls Yeats in "Sailing to Byzantium":

> An aged man is but a paltry thing,
> A tattered coat upon a stick, unless
> Soul clap its hands and sing, and louder sing
> For every tatter in its mortal dress.

When we for Age could neither read nor write,
The Subject made us able to indite.
The Soul with Nobler Resolutions deckt,
The Body stooping, does Herself erect:
5 No Mortal Parts are requisite to raise
Her, that Unbody'd can her Maker praise.

The Seas are quiet, when the Winds give o're;
So calm are we, when Passions are no more:
For then we know how vain it was to boast
10 Of fleeting Things, so certain to be lost.
Clouds of Affection from our younger Eyes
Conceal that emptiness, which Age descries.

The Soul's dark Cottage, batter'd and decay'd,
Lets in new Light thro chinks that time has made.
15 Stronger by weakness, wiser Men become
As they draw near to their Eternal home:
Leaving the Old, both Worlds at once they view,
That stand upon the Threshold of the New.

6 *Her . . . praise:* i.e. the soul, which raises itself as the body stoops in age (a variation on Donne's idea in l. 30 of "Hymne to God my God, in my sicknesse") and can survive the flesh which is unneeded to praise God.

C

Sir John Suckling

SONG: "OUT UPON IT, I HAVE LOV'D"

THERE IS a gay impudence in this song, mocking the whole Petrarchan tradition of chivalry, constancy and unrequited love, which clearly shows the influence on the Cavalier poets of Donne's early love poems in *Songs and Sonnets*. Aubrey called Suckling (1609–42) "the greatest gallant of his time". The abruptness of the short lines here gives an impact of reality to the feeling at the end, where after the flippant lightness of the first two verses the last two more seriously communicate his response to the perfection of "that very Face" which has commanded even this limited constancy.

Out upon it, I have lov'd,
Three whole days together;
And am like to love three more,
If it prove fair weather.

5 Time shall moult away his wings
Ere he shall discover
In the whole wide world agen
Such a constant Lover.

But the spite on't is, no praise
10 Is due at all to me:
Love with me had made no staies,
Had it any been but she.

Had it any been but she
And that very Face,
15 There had been at least ere this
A dozen dozen in her place.

11 *had made no staies:* would not have stayed with me, i.e. I would not have gone on loving.

William Cartwright

TO *CHLOE* WHO WISH'D HER SELF YOUNG ENOUGH FOR ME

THIS poem by William Cartwright (1611–43), on the theme of a disparity in age between lovers, is a novel reversal of the situation more usually depicted. Here it is his mistress who is older than the speaker; and Cartwright's graceful and witty persuasion that she should not be troubled by this explores one of Donne's favourite ideas of lovers attaining a harmony so complete that their souls are united. Love "makes two not alike, but One", and this fusion into a single being resolves the difference in their physical ages.

> *Chloe*, why wish you that your years
>   Would backwards run, till they meet mine,
> That perfect Likeness, which endears
>   Things unto things, might us Combine?
> 5 Our Ages so in date agree,
> That Twins do differ more than we.
>
> There are two Births, the one when Light
>   First strikes the new awak'ned sense;
> The Other when two Souls unite;
> 10   And we must count our life from thence:
> When you lov'd me, and I lov'd you,
> Then both of us were born anew.
>
> Love then to us did new Souls give,
>   And in those Souls did plant new pow'rs;
> 15 Since when another life we live,

The Breath we breathe is his, not ours;
Love makes those young, whom Age doth Chill,
And whom he finds young, keeps young still.

Love, like that Angell that shall call
20   Our bodies from the silent Grave,
Unto one Age doth raise us all,
     None too much, none too little have;
Nay that the difference may be none,
He makes two not alike, but One.

25   And now since you and I are such,
     Tell me what's yours, and what is mine?
Our Eyes, our Ears, our Taste, Smell, Touch,
     Do (like our Souls) in one Combine;
So by this, I as well may be
30   Too old for you, as you for me.

---

5 *Our Ages . . . agree:* in terms of their second "birth" when (l. 9) "two Souls unite".

16 *The Breath . . . ours:* See footnote to l. 26, "A Valediction: of Weeping", p. 17).

27–8 *Our Eyes . . . Combine:* Cf. again l. 26, "A Valediction: of Weeping".

Richard Crashaw

UPON THE DEATH OF A GENTLEMAN

PUBLISHED in 1646, this elegy on Michael Chambers, Fellow of Queens' College, is one of a group of funeral poems Crashaw wrote soon after going up to Cambridge in 1631. Its epigrammatic concentration and polish owe much to his early training in rhetoric during his schooldays at Charterhouse. T. S. Eliot said that Crashaw "might still have been a notable poet had he written no religious verse"; and this early piece is an accomplished exercise in the type of impersonal elegy which was a popular vehicle for wit. Built on a series of antitheses, it explores the idea of death's "reckoning" through a recurring metaphor of accountancy (ll. 2, 5, 24, 26, 31). The climactic conceit, of the eloquence of tears surpassing that of words, is a favourite metaphysical image (cf. Donne's "A Valediction: of Weeping", Marvell's "Eyes and Tears", Thomas Vaughan's "The Stone", and many of Crashaw's own poems, which anticipate the sustaining figure of his famous long poem "The Weeper").

> Faithlesse and fond Mortality,
> Who will ever credit thee?
> Fond and faithlesse thing! that thus,
> In our best hopes beguilest us.
> 5   What a reckoning hast thou made,
> Of the hopes in him we laid?
> For Life by volumes lengthened,
> A Line or two, to speake him dead.
> For the Laurell in his verse,
> 10   The sullen Cypresse o're his Herse.
> For a silver-crowned Head,
> A durty pillow in Death's Bed.

> For so deare, so deep a trust,
> Sad requitall, thus much dust!
> 15   Now though the blow that snatcht him hence,
> Stopt the Mouth of Eloquence,
> Though shee be dumbe e're since his Death,
> Not us'd to speake but in his Breath,
> Yet if at least shee not denyes,
> 20   The sad language of our eyes,
> Wee are contented: for then this
> Language none more fluent is.
> Nothing speakes our Griefe so well
> As to speake Nothing, Come then tell
> 25   Thy mind in Teares who e're Thou be,
> That ow'st a Name to misery.
> Eyes are vocall, Teares have Tongues,
> And there be words not made with lungs;
> Sententious showers, O let them fall,
> 30   Their cadence is Rhetoricall.
> Here's a Theame will drinke th'expence,
> Of all thy watry Eloquence,
> Weepe then, onely be exprest
> Thus much, *Hee's Dead,* and weepe the rest.

1 *Faithlesse and fond:* faithless to the dead man and his friends; "fond" perhaps in the double sense of "foolish", to cut off such a life, and "loving" in claiming him for itself.

2 *credit:* trust.

4 *beguilest:* deceives.

5 *reckoning:* account.

11 *For a silver-crowned Head:* For a life continuing till old age.

21 *then:* than.

22 *fluent:* a pun, on the fluency of language which flows in tears.

23-4 *Nothing . . . Nothing:* a typically metaphysical paradox.

24 *tell:* count.

29 *Sententious:* not in the modern meaning of "trite" or "pompous" but of "eloquently expressive".

30 *Their . . . Rhetoricall:* cf. Milton, "The Passion", st. vii:
> For sure so well instructed are my tears,
> That they would fitly fall in order'd Characters.

John Cleveland

THE ANTIPLATONICK

ONE of the most popular poets of the mid-seventeenth century, John Cleveland (1613–58) made his reputation as an extravagant wit and deadly political satirist. The irreverent cynicism of his argument against the Platonic ideal of love and its abstinence from physical union is epitomized in ll. 3–4. The inventive energy of the rapid succession of conceits which are the instruments of his mockery, the epigrammatic impact of the images in, for example, l. 16 and ll. 47–8, and the bold use of language in "eunuch" employed as a verb (l. 46), are characteristic of metaphysical wit at its most audacious, sophisticated and ingeniously fantastic.

> For shame, thou everlasting Wooer,
> Still saying grace, and never falling to her!
> Love that's in contemplation plac't,
> Is *Venus* drawn but to the wast.
> 5 Unlesse your flame confesse its gender,
> And your Parley cause surrender
> Y'are Salamanders of a cold desire
> That live untoucht amid the hottest fire.
>
> What though she be a Dame of stone
> 10 The Widow of *Pigmalion*;
> As hard and un-relenting she,
> As the new-crusted *Niobe*;
> Or what doth more of statue carry,
> A Nunne of the Platonick Quarry!
> 15 Love melts the rigour which the rocks have bred,
> A flint will break upon a Feather-bed.

For shame you pretty Female Elves
Cease for to candy up your selves:
No more, you sectaries of the Game,
20   No more of your calcining flame.
Women commence by *Cupids* Dart
As a King hunting dubs a Hart,
Loves votaries inthrall each others soul,
Till both of them live but upon Parole.

25   Vertue's no more in Woman-kind
But the green sicknesse of the mind.
Philosophy, their new delight,
A kind of Char-coal appetite.
There's no Sophistry prevails
30   Where all-convincing love assails;
But the disputing petticoat will warp
As skillfull gamesters are to seeke at sharp.

The souldier, that man of iron,
Whom ribs of *Horror* all inviron;
35   That's strung with Wire, instead of Veins,
In whose embraces you're in chains,
Let a Magnetick girl appear,
Straight he turns *Cupids* Cuirasseer,
Love storms his lips, and takes the Fortresse in,
40   For all the Bristled Turn-pikes of his chin.

Since Loves Artillery then checks
The brest-works of the firmest sex,
Come let us in affections riot,
Th'are sickly pleasures keep a Diet:
45   Give me a lover bold and free,
Not Eunucht with formality;
Like an Embassadour that beds a Queen
With the nice Caution of a sword between.

2 *saying grace:* as before a meal.
7 *Salamanders:* lizard-like reptiles once supposed to have the power of living in fire.

10 *The Widow of* Pigmalion: Cleveland envisages Pigmalion's widow reverting to stone on the death of her husband (cf. Ovid, *Met.* x, 243 ff.).

12 *the new-crusted* Niobe: a woman of Greek myth who was changed into a stone fountain while weeping for her children who had been killed (Ovid, *Met.* vi, 146–312).

18 *candy up your selves:* preserve yourselves in syrup.

19 *you sectaries of the Game:* lovers of the Platonic sect.

20 *calcining:* simultaneously, purifying or refining by consuming the grosser part; and reducing love to nothing but dust.

21–2 *Women . . . Hart:* i.e. Women graduate ("commence") through love in the same way as a hart is ennobled ("dubbed") by being hunted by a king.

24 *Parole:* literally the word of honour given by a prisoner that he will not escape; here in a second sense also—that the platonic lovers express their feelings only by words.

26 *green sicknesse:* i.e. an anaemic disease in adolescent girls often characterized by some morbid (here "Char-coal") appetite.

31–2 *But the disputing . . . sharp:* i.e. But the argumentative female will be bent or twisted from her natural form in the same way as clever fencers are unskilful in a real duel (a "sharp" was a small sword or duelling rapier).

37–8 *Let a . . . Cuirasseer:* A cuirass was a piece of body armour made of metal. Wearing this, the soldier would be irresistibly attracted to the "Magnetick girl".

40 *Turn-pikes:* spiked barriers fixed across a road to repel sudden attack.

44 *Th'are . . . Diet:* cf. l. 2.

Richard Lovelace

TO *ALTHEA*, FROM PRISON

IN the best poems of Richard Lovelace (1618–56/7) Grierson sees "the finest expression of honour and chivalry in all the Cavalier poetry of the century, the only poems which suggest what 'Cavalier' came to mean when glorified by defeat". This, the best known and most popular with his contemporaries of Lovelace's poems, was written in 1642 when he was imprisoned in the Gatehouse after presenting to the Commons the Kentish Petition for restoring the King to his rights. It is a moving affirmation of the liberties of mind and spirit defiantly undaunted by physical captivity.

> When Love with unconfined wings
>   Hovers within my Gates;
> And my divine *Althea* brings
>   To whisper at the Grates:
> 5 When I lye tangled in her haire,
>   And fetterd to her eye;
> The *Gods* that wanton in the Aire,
>   Know no such Liberty.
>
> When flowing Cups run swiftly round
> 10   With no allaying *Thames*,
> Our carelesse heads with Roses bound,
>   Our hearts with Loyall Flames;
> When thirsty griefe in Wine we steepe,
>   When Healths and draughts go free,
> 15 Fishes that tipple in the Deepe,
>   Know no such Libertie.

When (like committed Linnets) I
    With shriller throat shall sing
The sweetnes, Mercy, Majesty,
20   And glories of my KING;
When I shall voyce aloud, how Good
    He is, how Great should be;
Inlarged Winds that curle the Flood,
    Know no such Liberty.

25 Stone Walls doe not a Prison make,
        Nor Iron bars a Cage;
    Minds innocent and quiet take
        That for an Hermitage;
    If I have freedome in my Love,
30   And in my soule am free;
    Angels alone that sore above
        Injoy such Liberty.

4 *Grates:* prison grating.

9–10 *flowing Cups* . . . Thames: i.e. wine unallayed by water (the Thames flowed past his prison).

12 *Loyall:* to the King.

17 *committed Linnets:* imprisoned linnets. They are said to sing more sweetly in captivity.

21–2 *When I shall . . . should be:* Having done just this was the cause of his captivity.

Abraham Cowley

THE SPRING

ABRAHAM COWLEY (1618–67), a close friend of Crashaw at Cambridge and author of a well-known elegy on him, is generally considered to be the last of the major Metaphysical poets (see Introduction, p. 11). It was because his tone and attitudes already anticipated the Augustan Age of Reason that Johnson found him "undoubtedly the best" of the school of Donne. As Grierson says, "His wit is far less bizarre and extravagant than much in Donne", but "also less passionate and imaginative . . . the central heat has died down". Instead of making a conventional comparison between the beauties of nature and those of his mistress which outshine them, this poem takes the more unusual form of a rebuke to the spring for remaining as fair as ever in the absence of her who, for the poet, brings the true season with her. Grierson sees in it "a characteristically different treatment of much the same theme" as Donne used in "To the Countess of Bedford" ("Madame, You have refin'd mee"), and focuses the contrast on ll. 47–8 here with Donne's

> to this place
> You are the season (Madame) you the day,
> 'Tis but a grave of spices, till your face
> Exhale them, and a thick close bud display.

Though you be absent here, I needs must say
The *Trees* as beauteous are, and *flowers* as gay,
  As ever they were wont to be;
  Nay the *Birds* rural musick too
5 Is as melodious and free,

As if they sung to pleasure you:
I saw a *Rose-Bud* o'pe this morn; I'll swear
The blushing *Morning* open'd not more fair.

How could it be so fair, and you away?
10   How could the *Trees* be beauteous, *Flowers* so gay?
    Could they remember but last year,
    How *you* did *Them*, *They* *you* delight,
    The sprouting leaves which saw you here,
    And call'd their *Fellows* to the sight,
15   Would, looking round for the same sight in vain,
Creep back into their silent *Barks* again.

Where ere you walk'd trees were as reverend made,
As when of old *Gods* dwelt in every shade.
    Is't possible they should not know,
20   What loss of honor they sustain,
    That thus they smile and flourish now,
    And still their former pride retain?
Dull *Creatures*! 'tis not without Cause that she,
Who fled the *God of wit*, was made a *Tree*.

25   In ancient times sure they much wiser were,
When they rejoyc'd the *Thracian* verse to hear;
    In vain did *Nature* bid them stay,
    When *Orpheus* had his song begun,
    They call'd their wondring *roots* away,
30   And bad them silent to him run.
How would those learned trees have followed you?
You would have drawn *Them*, and their *Poet* too.

But who can blame them now? for, since you're gone,
They're here the *only Fair*, and *Shine alone*.
35   You did their *Natural Rights* invade;
    Where ever you did walk or sit,
    The thickest Boughs could make no *shade*,
    Although the Sun had granted it:
The fairest *Flowers* could please no more, neer you,
40   Then *Painted Flowers*, set next to them, could do.

When e're then you come hither, that shall be
The time, which this to others is, to *Me.*
   The little joys which here are now,
   The name of Punishments do bear;
45   When by their sight they let us know
   How we depriv'd of greater are.
'Tis you the best of *Seasons* with you bring;
This is for *Beasts,* and that for *Men* the *Spring.*

17–18 *Where ere . . . shade:* Cf. Pope, *Pastorals* "Summer" ll. 73–4

23–4 *'tis not . . .* Tree: Daphne, daughter of the river god Peneus, was pursued by Apollo and saved from him by being changed into a laurel tree.

25–30 *In ancient times . . . run:* Orpheus, the Thracian poet of Greek myth, enchanted the trees and rocks of Olympus so that they followed the music of his lyre.

Andrew Marvell

TO HIS COY MISTRESS

ANDREW MARVELL (1621–78) was one of the few poets of the period who supported the Puritan cause. He nevertheless numbered among his friends not only Milton (to whom he became assistant in the Latin Secretaryship in 1657 and defended from persecution in 1660) but also ardent Royalists like Lovelace and his own Cambridge contemporary, Cowley; and the blend in his work of moral seriousness with elegant urbanity combined the best of Puritan and Cavalier influences. In his best-known poem his powerful poetic individuality ingeniously revitalizes the familiar theme of *Carpe diem*. Here his strong affinities with Donne emerge in the vigorous directness of his address to the reluctant lady; his fusion of strong feeling with the ironical wit which intensifies it; and the close-knit, argumentative structure (what Eliot called a "tough reasonableness") of the "If" . . . "But" . . . "Therefore" dialectic of the poem's three contrasted paragraphs. In the first, the placing of human love in the large perspectives of time and space vividly recalls Donne, as does the vision of death and dissolution in the second. The opening passage of hyperbolical compliment to his mistress's beauty (which echoes a poem from Cowley's *The Mistress*: "My Dyet", stanza 3) moves at a measured, almost meditative pace; and the tempo accelerates until, by the end, the effect of impetuous speed in the short syllables and tight octosyllabic couplets communicates the impassioned urgency of the poet's plea to outrun "Times winged Charriot".

> Had we but World enough, and Time,
> This coyness Lady were no crime.
> We would sit down, and think which way
> To walk, and pass our long Loves Day.
> 5   Thou by the *Indian Ganges* side

Should'st Rubies find: I by the Tide
Of *Humber* would complain. I would
Love you ten years before the Flood:
And you should if you please refuse
10   Till the Conversion of the *Jews*.
My vegetable Love should grow
Vaster than Empires, and more slow.
An hundred years should go to praise
Thine Eyes, and on thy Forehead Gaze.
15   Two hundred to adore each Breast:
But thirty thousand to the rest.
An Age at least to every part,
And the last Age should show your Heart.
For Lady you deserve this State;
20   Nor would I love at lower rate.
    But at my back I alwaies hear
Times winged Charriot hurrying near:
And yonder all before us lye
Desarts of vast Eternity.
25   Thy Beauty shall no more be found;
Nor, in thy marble Vault, shall sound
My ecchoing Song: then Worms shall try
That long preserv'd Virginity:
And your quaint Honour turn to dust;
30   And into ashes all my Lust.
The Grave's a fine and private place,
But none I think do there embrace.
    Now therefore, while the youthful hew
Sits on thy skin like morning dew,
35   And while thy willing Soul transpires
At every pore with instant Fires,
Now let us sport us while we may;
And now, like am'rous birds of prey,
Rather at once our Time devour,
40   Than languish in his slow-chapt pow'r.
Let us roll all our Strength, and all
Our sweetness, up into one Ball:

> And tear our Pleasures with rough strife,
> Thorough the Iron gates of Life.
> 45 Thus, though we cannot make our Sun
> Stand still, yet we will make him run.

7 Humber: Note the effective juxtaposition of the homeliness of his native river (Marvell was a Yorkshireman) with the exotic image of rubies by the Ganges.

10 *the Conversion of the* Jews: According to ancient tradition this would take place immediately before the Day of Judgment.

11 *My vegetable Love:* The "vegetable" possesses the twin powers of growing and reproducing itself.

20 *at lower rate:* more cheaply.

21-4 *But . . . Eternity:* Tennyson found this vision of eternity "sublime". Grierson calls "the sudden soar of passion" in these "clangorous lines . . . the very roof and crown of the metaphysical love lyric, at once fantastic and passionate". The full sonority of l. 24, lost in modern spelling and pronunciation, was reinforced in Marvell's day by the assonance of "desarts", "vast" and "Eternity".

29 *Honour:* Pierre Legouis comments on the concrete use of the word as a sexual conceit, echoed by the Shakespearian meaning of "embrace" (l. 32).

40 *his . . . pow'r:* The "chaps" (or "chops") are the jaws of Time, which slowly devour human life.

44 *Thorough:* through.

45-6 *Thus . . . run:* The final paradox expresses still more strongly the defiant challenge to Time in ll. 39-40.

THE DEFINITION OF LOVE

"Whilst Mathematics were of late in vogue," wrote Thomas Blount in 1654, "all similitudes came from Lines, Circles and Angles". Marvell's interest in the sciences which preoccupied men of his day is skilfully exploited in the metaphysical wit of this love poem. Its astronomical images of celestial poles and stars, the cartographic metaphor of the planisphere or astrolabe, and the geometry of oblique and parallel lines effectively express the impossibility of uniting "two perfect Loves" because this opposes the decree of Fate embodied in every law of physical reality (ll. 15-16). Thus in the second verse "Magnanimous Despair" is seen as a higher thing, in plainly presenting an unattainable ideal, than the feeble, flimsy and counterfeit ("Tinsel") promises of Hope. The influence of Donne is even more apparent here, in the "bright, hard precision" (Eliot) of thought and metaphor and the interpretation of human love in terms of its cosmological setting. Pierre Legouis has called Marvell "an impassioned logician" in verse. This description well conveys his gift of charging deductive reasoning, paradoxical argument and learned imagery with the emotional intensity which makes this poem so much more than a mere arid exercise in wit.

My Love is of a birth as rare
As 'tis for object strange and high:
It was begotten by despair
Upon Impossibility.

5　Magnanimous Despair alone
Could show me so divine a thing,
Where feeble Hope could ne'r have flown
But vainly flapt its Tinsel Wing.

And yet I quickly might arrive
10　Where my extended Soul is fixt,
But Fate does Iron wedges drive,
And alwaies crouds it self betwixt.

For Fate with jealous Eye does see
Two perfect Loves; nor lets them close:
15　Their union would her ruine be,
And her Tyrannick pow'r depose.

And therefore her Decrees of Steel
Us as the distant Poles have plac'd,
(Though Loves whole World on us doth wheel)
20　Not by themselves to be embrac'd.

Unless the giddy Heaven fall,
And Earth some new Convulsion tear;
And, us to joyn, the World should all
Be cramp'd into a *Planisphere*.

25 As Lines so Loves *oblique* may well
   Themselves in every Angle greet:
   But ours so truly *Paralel*,
   Though infinite can never meet.

   Therefore the Love which us doth bind,
30 But Fate so enviously debarrs,
   Is the Conjunction of the Mind,
   And Opposition of the Stars.

10 *my extended Soul:* reaching up towards its "high object" (l. 2).

18 *the distant Poles:* the two poles of heaven.

20 *by themselves:* by each other.

21-4 *Unless . . . Planisphere:* i.e. Unless the vault of these celestial poles falls upon the earth, doing violence to Nature; and in order to join us the whole world is flattened into an astrolabe. This was a round plate on which the two sides showed the two hemispheres: "called of some a Planisphere," says a contemporary description, "because it is both flat and round, representing the Globe or Spheare, having both his Poles clapt flat together."

25-8 *As Lines . . . meet:* Grierson singles out these lines as "perfect exponents of the metaphysical qualities". The preceding stanza's image of the projection of half the globe on to a plane, with the meridians shown as straight lines intersecting at either pole, leads by natural association to the geometry of this one. While oblique lines, and loves less perfectly matched, always meet in an angle, the truly parallel, though infinite in extent, can never come together.

29-32 *Therefore . . . Stars:* Here is another close adaptation both in idea and imagery from Cowley ("Impossibilities", stanza 3). "Conjunction", the state of being in apparent union of heavenly bodies, and "Opposition", the situation of two heavenly bodies diametrically opposed, were familiar astronomical terms. The final line also carries the less specific meaning of "the opposition of Fate". Thus the situation of the lovers represents the paradox of a spiritual union whose geometry makes their physical separation a natural necessity.

Thomas Stanley

THE REPULSE

LIKE Cartwright's poem on p. 57, this one by Thomas Stanley (1625–78) presents another unusual aspect of love. The rejected suitor thinks himself fortunate, not in his future freedom either from loving the lady or to turn to others, but in the fact that she has never loved him. His banishment from that love would have caused him greater pain than his mere repulse after her inconstant favours. The freshness of this response to a conventional situation and the effective directness of the language reach a telling climax in the final paradox.

Not that by this disdain
I am releas'd,
And freed from thy tyrannick chain,
Do I my self think blest;

5   Not that thy Flame shall burn
No more; for know
That I shall into ashes turn,
Before this fire doth so.

Nor yet that unconfin'd
10   I now may rove,
And with new beauties please my mind;
But that thou ne'r didst love:

For since thou hast no part
Felt of this flame,
15 I onely from thy tyrant heart
Repuls'd, not banish'd am.

To lose what once was mine
Would grieve me more
Than those inconstant sweets of thine
20   Had pleas'd my soul before.

Now I have lost the blisse
I ne'r possest
And spight of fate am blest in this,
That I was never blest.

II: DIVINE POEMS

Sir Walter Ralegh

THE PASSIONATE MANS PILGRIMAGE, SUPPOSED TO BE WRITTEN BY ONE AT THE POINT OF DEATH

BORN twenty years earlier than Donne (although both sailed in 1596 in the Essex expedition to Cadiz), Ralegh (1552?–1618) was one of the great figures of the preceding Elizabethan age. This skilfully sustained conceit of his pilgrimage to heaven does, however, strikingly anticipate the manner of the Metaphysicals: in some places of Donne and Herbert (verses 5 and 6) and in others (verses 2, 3 and 4) of Crashaw. The poem was written when Ralegh was imprisoned for treason and under sentence of death at the end of 1603. He was later reprieved and spent twelve years in the Tower, where he wrote his *History of the World*.

> Give me my Scallop shell of quiet,
> My staffe of Faith to walke upon,
> My Scrip of Joy, Immortall diet,
> My bottle of salvation:
> 5   My Gowne of Glory, hopes true gage,
> And thus Ile take my pilgrimage.
>
> Blood must be my bodies balmer,
> No other balme will there be given
> Whilst my soule like a white Palmer
> 10   Travels to the land of heaven,
> Over the silver mountaines,
> Where spring the Nectar fountaines:
> And there Ile kisse
> The Bowle of blisse,

15 And drinke my eternall fill
   On every milken hill.
   My soule will be a drie before,
   But after, it will nere thirst more.

   And by the happie blisfull way
20 More peacefull Pilgrims I shall see,
   That have shooke off their gownes of clay,
   And goe appareld fresh like mee.
   Ile bring them first
   To slake their thirst
25 And then to taste those Nectar suckets
   At the cleare wells
   Where sweetnes dwells,
   Drawne up by Saints in Christall buckets.

   And when our bottles and all we,
30 Are fild with immortalitie:
   Then the holy paths wee'le travell
   Strewde with Rubies thicke as gravell,
   Ceelings of Diamonds, Saphire floores,
   High walles of Corall and Pearl Bowres.

35 From thence to heavens Bribeles hall
   Where no corrupted voyces brall,
   No Conscience molten into gold,
   Nor forg'd accusers bought and sold,
   No cause deferd, nor vaine spent Journey,
40 For there Christ is the Kings Atturney:
   Who pleades for all without degrees,
   And he hath Angells, but no fees.

   When the grand twelve million Jury
   Of our sinnes with sinfull fury,
45 Gainst our soules blacke verdicts give,
   Christ pleades his death, and then we live,
   Be thou my speaker taintles pleader,
   Unblotted Lawyer, true proceeder,

Thou movest salvation even for almes:
50   Not with a bribed Lawyers palmes.

And this is my eternall plea,
To him that made Heaven, Earth and Sea,
Seeing my flesh must die so soone,
And want a head to dine next noone,
55   Just at the stroke when my vaines start and spred
Set on my soule an everlasting head.
Then am I readie like a palmer fit,
To tread those blest paths which before I writ.

1–6 *Give me . . . pilgrimage:* The opening image is that of the medieval pilgrim, who in token of having travelled to the Holy Land carried a palm-leaf or -branch, from which his name "palmer" derived. He wore a belted gown (l. 5), and his other traditional equipment was a cockle- or scallop-shell (as a sign that he had visited the shrine of St. James of Compostella in Spain), a staff, a scrip (a small wallet or satchel), and a dried gourd-shell used as a water-bottle (l. 4).

7 *Blood . . . balmer:* i.e. The blood (of my execution) must purchase the peace of my body.

16 *milken hill:* an allusion to the promised land of milk and honey.

21 *gownes of clay:* the flesh.

25 *suckets:* sweets—usually fruit candied in syrup.

32–4 *Strewde . . . Bowres:* Cf. the vision of heaven in *Revelation* xxi, 18–21.

35–50 *From thence . . . palmes:* This legal metaphor of court and trial—which springs direct from Ralegh's own recent bitter experience—contrasts the corruptions of human justice with the incorruptibility and mercy of heaven.

37 *Conscience . . . gold:* conscience bribed with money.

41 *without degrees:* i.e. pleads for all without making distinctions and irrespective of their degrees of worldly importance or social standing; and perhaps simultaneously as a pun, viz. "without having law"—echoing the contempt for lawyers in ll. 35–8.

50 *palmes:* a pun, on the lawyer's itching palm and the palmer's badge.

54–6 *And want . . . everlasting head:* a grim (and peculiarly Metaphysical) reference to his anticipated death on the block.

58 *To tread . . . writ:* i.e. to tread in reality the heavenly paths which formerly I wrote about.

John Donne

HOLY SONNET: "BATTER MY HEART, THREE PERSON'D GOD; FOR, YOU"

ONE of Donne's "Holy Sonnets", a series of meditations on sin, death, judgment and the love of God, this poem derives its imaginative energy from the powerful use of paradox. The ideas of freedom through imprisonment and enslavement, and chastity through spiritual ravishment, support the central paradox of his religion on which the poem rests: "That I may rise, and stand, o'erthrow mee" (cf. the climactic thought in the next poem, "Hymne to God my God, in my sicknesse": "Therfore that he may raise the Lord throws down"). Donne envisages his soul in a state of willing siege by God, and sustains the metaphor of a town usurped by enemy violence which can be won back only by counter-violence in the total overthrow which he implores. There is a fierceness of feeling communicated by the impact of harsh onomatopoeic words like "batter", "knocke", "breake"; by the impetuous, flexible rhythms with their subtle variations of emphasis; and by the analogies of forcible possession culminating in the audacity, in the last line, of an erotic metaphor in this religious context. Thus Donne suggests not only that Divine love must storm the citadel of the spirit rather than gently woo ("breathe, shine, and seeke to mend") if it is to prove irresistible, but that it is an essentially similar invasion of the self to that of human love. He entreats God now with the ardour and passionate intensity of his earlier addresses to his "profane mistresses" and to his wife.

> Batter my heart, three person'd God; for, you
> As yet but knocke, breathe, shine, and seeke to mend;
> That I may rise, and stand, o'erthrow mee, 'and bend
> Your force, to breake, blowe, burn and make me new.

5 I, like an usurpt towne, to'another due,
  Labour to'admit you, but Oh, to no end,
  Reason your viceroy in mee, mee should defend,
  But is captiv'd, and proves weake or untrue,
  Yet dearely'I love you, and would be lov'd faine,
10 But am betroth'd unto your enemie,
  Divorce mee, 'untie, or breake that knot againe,
  Take mee to you, imprison mee, for I
  Except you'enthrall mee, never shall be free,
  Nor ever chast, except you ravish mee

1 *three person'd God:* the Trinity.
5 *to'another due:* owed to another—i.e. to God.
7 *Reason . . . mee:* Reason, ruling as God's deputy in me.
9 *would be lov'd faine:* wish to be loved.
10 *your enemie:* Satan.
11 *that knot:* of betrothal to sin.
13 *Except you'enthrall mee:* Unless you enslave me. T. S. Eliot calls the last two lines "in the best sense, *wit*".

HOLY SONNET: "DEATH BE NOT PROUD, THOUGH SOME HAVE CALLED THEE"

THIS is another of Donne's "Holy Sonnets", which Wordsworth thought "very fine". Here he defiantly challenges what in a sermon of 1621 he calls "the last and in that respect the worst enemy", and proclaims the ultimate invincibility of man's immortal soul. His arguments minimizing the tyrant's alleged power rise to their climax in the decisive statement of the concluding couplet, where his triumphant affirmation of the Christian victory in death's defeat by the resurrection of the spirit strikes home with monosyllabic force and finality.

  Death be not proud, though some have called thee
  Mighty and dreadfull, for, thou art not soe,
  For, those, whom thou think'st, thou dost overthrow,
  Die not, poore death, nor yet canst thou kill mee;

5 From rest and sleepe, which but thy pictures bee,
  Much pleasure, then from thee, much more must flow,
  And soonest our best men with thee doe goe,
  Rest of their bones, and soules deliverie.
  Thou art slave to Fate, chance, kings, and desperate men,
10 And dost with poyson, warre, and sicknesse dwell,
  And poppie, or charmes can make us sleepe as well,
  And better then thy stroake; why swell'st thou then?
  One short sleepe past, wee wake eternally,
  And death shall be no more, Death thou shalt die.

5–6 *From rest . . . flow:* i.e. From rest and sleep, which are only portrayals or imitations of death, men derive much pleasure; so it follows that from the reality much more must result.

7 *And soonest . . . goe:* referring either to the proverb that those loved by the gods die young, or the idea expressed in "A Valediction: forbidding mourning", ll. 1–2, of the ease and acceptance with which good men die.

8 *Rest . . . deliverie:* i.e. Their bodies find rest, their souls "delivery"— rebirth into immortality—from the body.

9 *Thou art . . . men:* i.e. Far from being a "mighty and dreadfull" despot, death is the mere slave of its own agents, circumstance and accident, kings who condemn men to die and the murderers or suicides ("desperate men") who inflict death.

12 *then thy stroake:* than thy stroke.

HYMNE TO GOD MY GOD, IN MY SICKNESSE

ACCORDING to Walton's biography this poem was written eight days before Donne's death in 1631, although another contemporary ascribes it to an earlier serious illness in December 1623, two years after his appointment as Dean of St. Paul's. It was first printed in 1635. In this meditation on the sufferings of his sick-bed and apparently imminent death, Donne's frequent sense of sin and tormented doubt give way to a less troubled hope of resurrection through the blood of "the last Adam". As in other poems (cf. especially "The Good-morrow" and "A Valediction: of Weeping"), Donne is keenly responsive to the temper of his time in employing metaphors from geographical exploration. Maps, cosmographers, and the evocative names of those distant territories which were then quickening public interest and imagination are used to interpret the experience of the spirit's final voyage of discovery. He envisages his body as a flat map of the world on which his doctors, like geographers, chart the course of his sickness. This image, with its striking idea of West (death) and East (resurrection) as one, is best explained in his own words in a sermon (*LXXX Sermons*, xxvii, 268): "In a flat Map, there goes no more, to make West East, though they be distant in an extremity, but to paste that flat Map upon a round body, and then West and East are all one."

Since I am comming to that Holy roome,
   Where, with thy Quire of Saints for evermore,
I shall be made thy Musique; As I come
   I tune the Instrument here at the dore,
5   And what I must doe then, thinke now before.

Whilst my Physitians by their love are growne
   Cosmographers, and I their Mapp, who lie
Flat on this bed, that by them may be showne
   That this is my South-west discoverie
10   *Per fretum febris*, by these streights to die,

I joy, that in these straits, I see my West;
   For, though theire currants yeeld return to none,
What shall my West hurt me? As West and East
   In all flatt Maps (and I am one) are one,
15   So death doth touch the Resurrection.

Is the Pacifique Sea my home? Or are
   The Easterne riches? Is *Jerusalem*?
Anyan, and *Magellan*, and *Gibraltare*,
   All streights, and none but streights, are wayes to them,
20   Whether where *Japhet* dwelt, or *Cham*, or *Sem*.

We thinke that *Paradise* and *Calvarie*,
   Christs Crosse, and *Adams* tree, stood in one place;
Looke Lord, and finde both *Adams* met in me;
   As the first *Adams* sweat surrounds my face,
25   May the last *Adams* blood my soule embrace.

So, in his purple wrapp'd receive mee Lord,
By these his thornes give me his other Crowne;
And as to others soules I preach'd thy word,
Be this my Text, my Sermon to mine owne,
30   Therfore that he may raise the Lord throws down.

4–5 *I tune . . . before:* i.e. Here on the threshold of death I prepare myself for the life to come.

9–10 *my South-west . . . die:* i.e. my death, in the heat of the South (my fever) and the West of the setting sun. There is a double pun here: *per fretum febris* means literally "through the strait of fever", but *fretum* also means "raging" (referring to his fever); and "strait" has the meaning of both "channel" and "distress".

16–17 *Is the Pacifique Sea . . . Is* Jerusalem?: Some medieval thinkers, like Dante, imagined the location of the Earthly Paradise in the Southern Ocean ("the Pacifique Sea"). Others placed it in the farthest East, beyond the fabled riches of Cathay. Donne's contemporaries shared the view that it was in Mesopotamia, the same part of the world as Jerusalem.

18–19 Anyan *. . . wayes to them:* The Anyan (or Behring) Straits lead to the far East, Magellan's Straits to the Pacific, and Gibraltar is the way to Jerusalem. Only through these straits of sickness and death—"a narrower way, but to a better land", as Donne said in a sermon—may the spirit reach its ultimate destination.

20 *Whether . . . Sem:* Old sketch-maps show the world divided between the sons of Noah. Japhet's portion was Europe, Ham's Africa, and Shem's Asia.

21–2 *We thinke . . . one place:* Ancient Christian tradition links the tree of Eden and the Cross. Referring back to Jerusalem, in the previous verse, Donne probably means by "one place" simply "in the same region"— i.e. Mesopotamia, the home of both Paradise and Calvary; and that the one may be reached only by way of the other.

26 *purple:* suggesting both the colour of kingly robes and of Christ's blood (see footnote to l. 9 of Marvell's "On a Drop of Dew", p. 140; also cf. Crashaw "On our crucified Lord Naked, and bloody", ll. 3–4: "Thee with thy selfe they have too richly clad,/Opening the purple wardrobe of thy side").

30 *Therfore . . . down:* Donne expresses the same thought in *Sermon* xxvi: "Man was fallen, and God took that way to raise him, to throw him lower, into the grave."

A HYMNE TO GOD THE FATHER

WALTON describes how Donne wrote this poem in his illness of 1623 and later caused it "to be set to a most grave and solemn Tune, and to be often sung to the *Organ* by the *Choristers* of St. *Paul's* Church, in his own hearing . . . and . . . did occasionally say to a friend, *The words of this* Hymn *have restored to me the same thoughts of joy that possest my Soul in my sickness when I composed it*". A setting by John Hilton, organist at St. Margaret's, Westminster, who died in 1657, is preserved in a manuscript in the British Museum. The recurring pun on his name in each stanza (emphasized by the spelling in some of the manuscript versions of the poem) recalls Donne's wry epigram on the disastrous consequences to his career of his marriage: "John Donne, Ann Donne—Undone" (see note to "The Canonization", l. 3, p. 34). It also strikingly illustrates the Metaphysical use of wit in a solemn context. Conceits and word-play were for Donne in no way inconsistent with high seriousness in the treatment of such subjects as sin and salvation. Here the reiterated double meaning intensifies both the concentration of his plea and the final resolution of his fear. Donne's theme is an urgently personal interpretation of the thought in *Romans* vi, 23: "For the wages of sin is death; but the gift of God is eternal life through Jesus Christ our Lord."

Wilt thou forgive that sinne where I begunne,
    Which is my sin, though it were done before?
Wilt thou forgive those sinnes through which I runne,
    And doe them still: though still I doe deplore?
5   When thou hast done, thou hast not done,
            For, I have more.

Wilt thou forgive that sinne by which I wonne
    Others to sinne? and, made my sinne their doore?
Wilt thou forgive that sinne which I did shunne
10   A yeare, or two: but wallowed in, a score?
        When thou hast done, thou hast not done,
            For, I have more.

I have a sinne of feare, that when I have spunne
My last thred, I shall perish on the shore;
15   Sweare by thy selfe, that at my death thy Sonne
Shall shine as he shines now, and heretofore;
And, having done that, Thou hast done,
I feare no more.

1–2 *that sinne . . . before?:* i.e. the original sin with which I began my life, which is still my sin, even though inherited and committed before my birth. Cf. *Psalm* li, 5: "Behold I was shapen in iniquity: and in sin did my mother conceive me."

5–6 *When thou hast done . . . more:* i.e. When you have finished (forgiving these sins), you do not possess me (Donne), for I have more.

7–8 *that sinne . . . doore:* possibly, as Helen Gardner suggests, the writing of licentious poetry. Cf. also *L Sermons*, xxxv, 319: "There shall fall upon him those sinnes which he hath done after another's dehortation, and those, which others have done after his provocation."

14 *thred:* of life; *the shore:* of death.

15 *Sweare by thy selfe:* Cf. God's promise to Abraham, *Gen.* xxii, 16: "By myself have I sworn, saith the Lord."

15–16 *that at my death . . . shines now:* A pun on "sun" and "Son". Cf. *L Sermons*, xxviii, 343: "I shall see the Sonne of God, the Sunne of glory, and shine my self, as that sunne shines." (Helen Gardner prefers the MS reading of "Sunne" to "Sonne" in the published text of 1633 adopted by Grierson and given here.)

16 *heretofore:* always from the beginning.

17 *Thou hast done:* i.e. You have finally finished and possess me wholly.

18 *feare:* Gardner gives the MS reading of "have" instead of the 1633 "feare" used by Grierson; although he allows that "have" (i.e. no more to ask and no more sins) emphasizes the recurring play on Donne's name, and that "I have no more" is equivalent to "I am Donne" (i.e. finished with asking).

Francis Quarles

ON ZACHEUS

FRANCIS QUARLES (1592–1644) was highly regarded as a religious poet in his own day, and his *Emblems* (1635) was one of the most popular books of verse of the century. The story of Zacchaeus (*Luke* xix, 2–6) is used here with a wider application to the whole nature of religious faith (ll. 5–8). The vigour of the verb "powder'd" suggests both the dust shaken from the tree and the mortal dust of which a man is made; and the metaphysical paradox in the magnificent l. 10, of the fall in order to rise, is an idea frequently expressed by Donne.

> Me thinks, I see, with what a busie hast,
> *Zacheus* climb'd the Tree: But, O, how fast,
> How full of speed, canst thou imagine (when
> Our *Saviour* call'd) he powder'd downe agen!
> 5 He ne're made tryall, if the boughs were sound,
> Or rotten; nor how far 'twas to the ground:
> There was no danger fear'd; At such a Call,
> Hee'l venture nothing, that dare feare a fall;
> Needs must hee downe, by such a *Spirit* driven;
> 10 Nor could he fall, unlesse he fell to *Heaven*:
> Downe came *Zacheus*, ravisht from the Tree;
> Bird that was shot ne're dropt so quicke as he.

George Herbert

AFFLICTION (I)

SON of Donne's friend Lady Magdalen Herbert (see headnote to "The Relique", p. 36), George Herbert (1593–1633) was like Donne disappointed in his ambitions for a career at Court. Probably encouraged by Donne, he took the same decision to enter the Church, and spent the last three years of his short life as a country parson at Bemerton, near Salisbury. *The Temple*, published a few months after his death, was much admired and reprinted throughout the century. According to Walton, whose life of Herbert was published in 1670, he sent his friend Nicholas Ferrar the manuscript as "a picture of the many spiritual Conflicts that have past betwixt God and my Soul, before I could subject mine to the will of Jesus my Master: in whose service I have now found perfect freedom". In this autobiographical poem "Affliction" (the first of five with the same title) Herbert movingly chronicles the various vicissitudes in the stages of his spiritual progress towards a final dedication to his calling. In its "masterly verse", says L. C. Knights in *Explorations*, "we have one of the most remarkable records in the language of the achievement of maturity and of the inevitable pains of the process". This is a self-portrait of a man who starts out on the Christian way in the unsuspecting hope and joyous confidence of youth, only to find himself gradually besieged by a succession of misfortunes—sickness, the death of friends, the loss of his youthful "mirth and edge" with that of the life to which his birth and spirit inclined him, and even denial of the opportunity for self-indulgence in his misery—so bitter and relentless that his faith is tried to breaking-point, and the "brave" service becomes a servitude. The recognition in "The Flower" of the reason for his suffering—that darkness is a necessity for light—has not yet been vouchsafed to him. Yet his impulse at the end of this poem to desert God for "some other master" is rejected as soon as contemplated. Bewildered and uncomprehending ("what thou wilt do with me/None of my books will show") in these storms of adversity

D

where "Sorrow was all [his] soul", he nerves himself to submit with patience
and fortitude and to continue to love even though he cannot understand.

When first thou didst entice to thee my heart,
        I thought the service brave:
So many joyes I writ down for my part,
        Besides what I might have
5   Out of my stock of naturall delights,
Augmented with thy gracious benefits.

I looked on thy furniture so fine,
        And made it fine to me:
Thy glorious houshold-stuffe did me entwine,
10   And 'tice me unto thee.
Such starres I counted mine: both heav'n and earth
Payd me my wages in a world of mirth.

What pleasures could I want, whose King I served,
        Where joyes my fellows were?
15   Thus argu'd into hopes, my thoughts reserved
        No place for grief or fear.
Therefore my sudden soul caught at the place,
And made her youth and fiercenesse seek thy face.

At first thou gav'st me milk and sweetnesses;
20   I had my wish and way:
My dayes were straw'd with flow'rs and happinesse;
        There was no moneth but May.
But with my yeares sorrow did twist and grow,
And made a partie unawares for wo.

25   My flesh began unto my soul in pain,
        Sicknesses cleave my bones;
Consuming agues dwell in ev'ry vein,
        And tune my breath to grones.
Sorrow was all my soul; I scarce beleeved,
30   Till grief did tell me roundly, that I lived.

When I got health, thou took'st away my life,
        And more; for my friends die:

My mirth and edge was lost; a blunted knife
    Was of more use than I.
35 Thus thinne and lean without a fence or friend,
    I was blown through with ev'ry storm and winde.

Whereas my birth and spirit rather took
    The way that takes the town;
Thou didst betray me to a lingring book,
40   And wrap me in a gown.
I was entangled in the world of strife,
Before I had the power to change my life.

Yet, for I threatned oft the siege to raise,
    Not simpring all mine age,
45 Thou often didst with Academick praise
    Melt and dissolve my rage.
I took thy sweetned pill, till I came where
I could not go away, nor persevere.

Yet lest perchance I should too happie be
50   In my unhappinesse,
Turning my purge to food, thou throwest me
    Into more sicknesses.
Thus doth thy power crosse-bias me, not making
Thine own gift good, yet me from my wayes taking.

55 Now I am here, what thou wilt do with me
    None of my books will show:
I reade, and sigh, and wish I were a tree;
    For sure then I should grow
To fruit or shade: at least some bird would trust
60 Her houshold to me, and I should be just.

Yet, though thou troublest me, I must be meek;
    In weaknesse must be stout.
Well, I will change the service, and go seek
    Some other master out.
65 Ah my deare God! though I am clean forgot,
Let me not love thee, if I love thee not.

1–2 *When first . . . brave:* Herbert had always been deeply religious, and at the age of seventeen sent his mother two sonnets dedicating his skill in the writing of poetry "to God's glory".

7–10 *I looked . . . unto thee:* Herbert may be using this characteristically homely imagery of God's "furniture" and "houshold-stuffe" in a double sense: for the natural beauty of creation surrounding him, and for the ceremonial equipment of the Church (cf. his prose *A Priest to the Temple, or, The Country Parson,* ch. XIII, "The Parson's Church"). Thus he enjoys in youth the benefits of "both heav'n and earth".

13 *What pleasures   serued:* i.e. What pleasures could I look, who serued the King of pleasures? George Williamson suggests that "The possible ambiguities of this stanza [ll. 13–18] might reflect a secular disappointment" as well as the obvious interpretation (*A Reader's Guide to the Metaphysical Poets,* p. 97).

17–18 *Therefore . . . face:* a fine evocation, in the words "sudden" (hasty) and "fiercenesse", of Herbert's impetuous temperament.

19–22 *At first . . . May:* L. C. Knights in *Explorations* comments on how, in these opening stanzas, "movement and imagery combine to evoke the enchanted world of early manhood. But implicit in the description—as we see from 'entice' and 'entwine' and the phrase 'argu'd into hopes'—is the admission that there *is* enchantment, an element of illusion."

25 *My flesh . . . pain:* i.e. began to say: so that the next three lines, with their verbs in the present tense, are the complaint of the flesh to the soul.

32 *my friends die:* Between 1624 and 1625 the deaths occurred of the Duke of Richmond, the Marquis of Hamilton, and James I, three of Herbert's most powerful patrons with whom, according to Walton, perished "all Mr. *Herbert's* Court-hopes". Bacon and Lancelot Andrewes died in 1626 and Herbert's mother in 1627. The loss of his influential friends precipitated his decision to take orders in 1626, and, as Walton puts it, change "his sword and silk Cloaths into a Canonical Coat".

37–8 *my birth . . . town:* my aristocratic birth and natural inclination led me towards a secular career. Herbert had hoped for an appointment as a Secretary of State. His first biographer, Barnabas Oley, interprets "the way that takes the town" as "Martiall Atchievements", but Hutchinson thinks it as likely to be what Walton calls "the painted pleasures of a Court life". The word "takes" may mean either (or perhaps simultaneously, as a pun) "the way, or course, the town takes", or "the way that attracts, or pleases, the town".

39–40 *Thou didst . . . gown:* i.e. the book and gown of the scholar. Herbert studied classics and divinity at Cambridge, was appointed Reader in Rhetoric in 1618, and Public Orator from 1620-7.

41-2 *I was entangled . . . life:* Empson comments: "Long as Herbert delayed in taking orders, the two halves of this verse [ll. 37-42], one saying he was *betrayed* into the life of contemplation, the other that he was *entangled* in the life of action, show him still doubtful which he would have preferred. Thus he seems to want to *change his life* even now, but it is hard to see in what direction" (*Seven Types of Ambiguity*, p. 183).

43 *for:* because.

43-8 *Yet . . . persevere:* Barnabas Oley interprets these lines: "that whereas his birth and spirit prompted him to . . . the way that takes the town; and not to sit simpering over a book; God did often melt his spirit, and entice him with academic honour, to be content to wear, and wrap up himself in a gown, so long, till he durst not put it off, nor retire to any other calling." In ll. 47-8 he has come to the state of mind where he could neither retreat from nor continue in his present way of life.

53 *crosse-bias me:* divert, turn me aside from my own inclination. The term is taken from the game of bowls.

57-60 *I reade . . . houshold to me:* Cf. the imagery of nature, and of his soul as a plant, throughout "The Flower"; *I should be just:* i.e. my existence would be justified.

63-4 *Well . . . out:* Cf. "The Collar", ll. 27-32. The words come as something of a shock after the apparent acquiescence of the two preceding lines.

65-6 *Ah my deare God! . . . love thee not:* This abrupt transition from rebellion to contrition, expressed in the form of an arresting paradox simultaneously affirming the impossibility of his desertion and shame at his own spiritual inadequacy, recalls the conclusion of "The Collar". Herbert is saying: "Though it may mean that you forget me completely, if I cannot love you without reservation for your own sake, in spite of the afflictions you send me, let me be released from loving you altogether." Empson suggests that the phrase "though I am clean forgot" may, in the light of the preceding lines, apply to his being forgotten either by God or by the world (see *Seven Types of Ambiguity*, pp. 183-4). F. E. Hutchinson paraphrases this "passionate return to the first and only allegiance possible to him" thus: "If he cannot hold on to his love of God even when he feels forsaken and unrewarded, he had better not hope to love at all" (*The Works of George Herbert*, Commentary, p. 492).

THE COLLAR

HERBERT probes in his work the complex moods and motives of his
religious experience with an honesty and subtlety of analysis comparable
to that which Donne brought to his love poems; and "The Collar" is his
most energetic expression of the rebellion of self-will against the disciplines
of his vocation. Its diction and verse-form, exactly suited to the poem's
content, exemplify what T. S. Eliot calls Herbert's "extraordinary metrical
virtuosity" and "resourcefulness of invention". The colloquial tone, staccato
phrases and reiterated peremptory demands of his angry self-questioning
and impassioned statement of grievance; the growing incoherence of the
images (e.g. the "cage" juxtaposed with the "rope of sands"); the forceful,
irregular movement of the metre, variations in length of line, and widely
spaced incidence of the rhymes, all brilliantly communicate the violence
of the speaker's struggle to break free from the constraint of the collar (a
symbol in common use by preachers for the discipline imposed by conscience
and religion). The rapid, impetuous urgency of speech seems to defy the
prescribed patterns of verse as of behaviour, until poetic order is finally
imposed upon the skilfully disordered rhythm and rhyme-scheme as these
subside into the regularity of the concluding four lines. Notice how the
Voice which brings the speaker to his senses needs to utter no more than
a single, subduing word of paternal rebuke to quell rebellion at its climax,
its quiet courtesy underlined by the noisy self-assertiveness of the protest.
The speaker's final submission and acknowledgment of authority are in
their simplicity as child-like as the petulant outburst is intended to be
recognized as childish.

> I struck the board, and cry'd, No more.
> I will abroad.
> What? shall I ever sigh and pine?
> My lines and life are free; free as the rode,
> 5 Loose as the winde, as large as store.
> Shall I be still in suit?
> Have I no harvest but a thorn
> To let me bloud, and not restore
> What I have lost with cordiall fruit?

10   Sure there was wine
      Before my sighs did drie it: there was corn
          Before my tears did drown it.
        Is the yeare onely lost to me?
        Have I no bayes to crown it?
15 No flowers, no garlands gay? all blasted?
           All wasted?
        Not so, my heart: but there is fruit,
          And thou hast hands.
      Recover all thy sigh-blown age
20 On double pleasures: leave thy cold dispute
      Of what is fit, and not. Forsake thy cage,
          Thy rope of sands,
      Which pettie thoughts have made, and made to thee
        Good cable, to enforce and draw,
25   And be thy law,
      While thou didst wink and wouldst not see.
          Away; take heed:
          I will abroad.
      Call in thy deaths head there: tie up thy fears.
30   He that forbears
        To suit and serve his need,
          Deserves his load.
      But as I rav'd and grew more fierce and wilde
         At every word,
35   Me thoughts I heard one calling, *Child!*
        And I reply'd, *My Lord.*

1 *the board:* the altar—God's table on which the bread and wine of the Sacrament are served. The abrupt dramatic shock of this opening line recalls Donne.

2 *I will abroad:* I will go out ("abroad" is obsolete in this sense).

4 *lines:* ways. Also by association the suggestion of "life-lines"—ropes used in rescue work at sea—contrasted with the futility of the "rope of sands" of l. 22.

5 *Loose as the winde:* The adjective significantly points the purposeless irresponsibility of the desired liberty; *as large as store:* as large as the plenty there for the taking.

6 *still in suit?:* always a suitor in another's (i.e. God's) service?

7–10 *Have I . . . wine:* These images of parable and sacrament—harvest, thorn, blood, wine—applied to himself in a secular sense echo the blasphemy of the opening line.

8 *To let me bloud:* blood-letting, the drawing off blood from a vein.

9 *cordiall:* reviving, stimulating.

14 *bayes:* the laurel garland worn by a hero or poet: an implicit contrast of this badge of worldly honour with the other crown, of thorn (l. 7).

15–16 *all blasted?/All wasted?:* laid waste by the cold wind of conscience.

19–20 *sigh-blown age . . . pleasures:* the obvious echo of "fly-blown" hints at coarse self-indulgence (cf. "loose", l. 5) as he contemplates making up for lost time.

20–6 *leave . . . see:* i.e. Leave your cold argument with conscience which has imprisoned you; your futile "rope of sands" which has made a "good cable" to bind and govern your life, while you were wilfully blinkered and refused to recognize the possibility of freedom.

27–8 *Away . . . abroad:* l. 2 is reiterated with the emphasis of a childishly defiant threat to the Almighty.

29 *deaths head:* the skull, emblem of mortality. i.e. I will cease to be constrained by that *memento mori*, and by fears of the life to come.

31 *suit:* an echo of the "suitor" image of l. 6; also a pun, in the colloquial sense of one who "suits himself" and serves his own need, not God's will.

33–4 *But . . . word:* the first explicit recognition of what has been implied throughout in the turbulence of language and metre: that his revolt has resembled the fierceness and wildness of an animal, the raving of a madman, each needing to be tamed by the restraint of the collar.

THE FLOWER

IN striking contrast with the brash, unmannerly accents of Herbert's defiant confrontation of God in the preceding poem is the serenity of his address in this meditation on his own inadequacies, which compares the aridity of alienation from grace with the peace and fulfilment of reconciliation. T. S. Eliot speaks of Herbert's "spiritual stamina". No less apparent in this poem is his quality of spiritual resilience: the ability to revive—and even appear to emerge renewed—from a depth of despondency bordering on despair. (It rewards study to compare "The Flower" with some of the poems written by Gerard Manley Hopkins, especially "Thou art indeed just, Lord" and "Carrion Comfort", out of a similar mood of barrenness and apparent desertion by God.) The epithets of the opening line—"fresh", "sweet", "clean"—apply with peculiar aptness to the purity and felicity of Herbert's language here: the intimate conversational ease, naturalness and simplicity of his colloquy with God and his quiet acceptance of the inevitability of periods of dryness and darkness for the human spirit, as in the cycle of nature, in order to enable the process of renewal. The sustained analogy of the seasons and weathers of the earth with those of one man's spiritual life, and the use of emotive words like "shrivel'd", "wither", and "spring-showre", vividly suggest the thirst of the parched spirit after righteousness. Aldous Huxley in *Texts and Pretexts* has noted how in Herbert "The climate of the mind is positively English in its variableness and instability", the "bewildering rapidity" of its changes, and how "Herbert is the poet of this inner weather". The lines of irregular lengths—the short rhymed couplets of the fifth and sixth lines of each stanza and the alternating rhymes in the longer lines—serve skilfully to reflect the writer's mood and situation.

How fresh, O Lord, how sweet and clean
Are thy returns! ev'n as the flowers in spring;
To which, besides their own demean,
The late-past frosts tributes of pleasure bring.
5   Grief melts away
         Like snow in May,
As if there were no such cold thing.

Who would have thought my shrivel'd heart
Could have recover'd greennesse? It was gone
10   Quite under ground; as flowers depart
To see their mother-root, when they have blown;
         Where they together
         All the hard weather,
Dead to the world, keep house unknown.

15   These are thy wonders, Lord of power,
Killing and quickning, bringing down to hell
         And up to heaven in an houre;
Making a chiming of a passing-bell.

We say amisse,
20   This or that is:
Thy word is all, if we could spell.

O that I once past changing were,
Fast in thy Paradise, where no flower can wither!
Many a spring I shoot up fair,
25 Offring at heav'n, growing and groning thither:
      Nor doth my flower
      Want a spring-showre,
My sinnes and I joining together.

But while I grow in a straight line,
30 Still upwards bent, as if heav'n were mine own,
Thy anger comes, and I decline:
What frost to that? what pole is not the zone,
      Where all things burn,
      When thou dost turn,
35 And the least frown of thine is shown?

And now in age I bud again,
After so many deaths I live and write;
I once more smell the dew and rain,
And relish versing: O my onely light,
40   It cannot be
      That I am he
On whom thy tempests fell all night.

These are thy wonders, Lord of love,
To make us see we are but flowers that glide:
45   Which when we once can finde and prove,
Thou hast a garden for us, where to bide.
      Who would be more,
      Swelling through store,
Forfeit their Paradise by their pride.

3-4 *To which . . . bring:* i.e. The spring flowers bring pleasure not only
in their own demeanour (and possibly also "demesne"—"estate, state of
life") but as a sign that the recent frosts of winter are past.

9–11 *It was gone . . . blown:* Cf. Donne, "A Hymne to Christ", ll. 13–16:

> As the trees sap doth seeke the root below
> In winter, in my winter now I goe,
> Where none but thee th'Eternall root
> Of true love I may know.

16–17 *Killing . . . houre:* The swift change in spiritual mood recalls Huxley's comment (above) on Herbert's mercurial inner climate. Cf. also Donne, "Hymne to God my God, in my sicknesse", l. 30: "Therfore that he may raise the Lord throws down."

18 *Making . . . passing-bell:* i.e. turning the slow, solemn sound of the funeral-bell, tolling on a single note, to the joyous sound of chiming bells.

19–21 *We say . . . spell:* i.e. We are mistaken if we say that any thing exists in itself unchangeably: it is made what it is only by virtue of God's law, if we could "spell" and read his word (*viz.* recognize this fact).

25 *Offring at:* reaching towards; *growing and groning:* alliteration and assonance suggest the painful effort of his striving after holiness.

26–8 *Nor doth . . . together:* i.e. Nor does my spirit's flower lack a spring shower, watered by the tears in which my sins and I join (note the effective internal half-rhyme of "joining" with "groning").

30 *upwards bent:* aiming at, bent on, heaven.

32–5 *What frost . . . shown?:* i.e. What frost can compare with God's anger? What cold polar region is not like the burning heat of the torrid zone beside his least frown?

36–42 *And now . . . all night:* T. S. Eliot calls this stanza "a miracle of phrasing", and A. Alvarez (*The School of Donne*) "the most perfect and the most vivid stanza in the whole of Herbert's work . . . so natural that its originality is easily missed".

36–7 *in age . . . so many deaths:* Herbert died in only his fortieth year, though having suffered "many deaths" of recurring ill-health as well as these moods of dejection and separation from grace.

39 *relish versing:* Coleridge singled out this "homely" phrase from a poem he found "especially affecting", for "a sincerity, a reality, which I would unwillingly exchange for the more dignified 'and once more love the Muse' &c." (Letter to William Collins, 6 December 1818).

43 *Lord of love:* a reiteration of l. 15 with the alteration of one word: "power" has become "love".

44 *glide:* pass, slip imperceptibly away.

45 *Which . . . prove:* when once we can perceive and experience this truth.

46 *bide:* abide, live perpetually.

47–8 *Who would . . . store:* i.e. those who would be more than transient earthly flowers created for the garden of "thy Paradise, where no flower can wither", increasing themselves through worldly plenty.

THE PULLEY

IN this poem Herbert re-creates in Christian terms the classical myth of the box of the blessings of the gods given by Jupiter to Pandora, the first mortal woman. The "jewel" of Pandora's box, which lay at the bottom while all the rest slipped out and were lost, was hope. In God's "glasse of blessings" it is rest, which he withholds from man as the incentive to seek him—using human restlessness as the pulley to draw his creature finally to himself in the same way as Herbert's play on the word "rest" acts as a verbal pulley throughout the poem.

> When God at first made man,
> Having a glasse of blessings standing by;
> Let us (said he) poure on him all we can;
> Let the worlds riches, which dispersed lie,
> 5   Contract into a span.
>
> So strength first made a way;
> Then beautie flow'd, then wisdome, honour, pleasure;
> When almost all was out, God made a stay,
> Perceiving that alone of all his treasure
> 10   Rest in the bottome lay.
>
> For if I should (said he)
> Bestow this jewell also on my creature,
> He would adore my gifts in stead of me,
> And rest in Nature, not the God of Nature:
> 15   So both should losers be.
>
> Yet let him keep the rest,
> But keep them with repining restlessnesse:
> Let him be rich and wearie, that at least,
> If goodnesse leade him not, yet wearinesse
> 20   May tosse him to my breast.

4–5 *Let . . . span:* i.e. Let life's riches, dispersed all over the world, be concentrated into the compass of each human life (cf. Donne's similar use of the verb "contract" in "The Sunne Rising", l. 26).

6 *made a way:* out of the glass, followed by the other blessings.

8 *God made a stay:* paused.

14 *And rest . . . God of Nature:* the heresy of pantheism.

15 *both:* God and man.

16 *the rest:* the remainder; but also a play on the word already used in ll. 10 and 14 in the sense of "repose", and here immediately followed by the opposition of "repining restlessnesse".

20 *tosse:* a strong verb suggesting movement, effort, the restless vigour of human search for a satisfaction beyond that offered by all the other blessings.

MAN

HERBERT meditates here upon a different aspect of man from the vacillations, rebellions and spiritual inadequacies he discerns in himself in "Affliction", "The Collar" and "The Flower", and from the restlessness which is the theme of "The Pulley". In this poem his conception of the human condition recalls Hamlet (II, ii) before the entrance of the players: "What a piece of work is a man! How noble in reason! how infinite in faculties! in form and moving, how express and admirable! in action, how like an angel! in apprehension, how like a god! the beauty of the world! the paragon of animals!" Marvelling at the wisdom and artistry with which the human reason, body and faculties have been framed by their creator to be "in little all the sphere . . . ev'ry thing/And more", and at the bounty of the blessings God has prepared for man's benefit, surrounding him on every side, Herbert also shares the mood of Traherne's exultant praises (see especially "The Salutation"). From sun and stars, moons and tides to the humble herbs beneath his feet, all creation conspires to minister to man and serve his needs on an earth where "Nothing we see, but means our good,/As our delight, or as our treasure". Here and there, however, comes an intimation that man may be liable to mar this God-given perfection: in the laconic "should be" of l. 9; the suggestion in ll. 44–5 that the very prodigality of man's blessings may make him indifferent or neglectful of them; and the closing invocation to God to inhabit his "brave Palace" and afford man enough sense (implying that he may not in himself possess "so much wit") to serve his maker and donor of the world which serves him.

My God, I heard this day,
That none doth build a stately habitation,
But he that means to dwell therein.
What house more stately hath there been,
5   Or can be, then is Man? to whose creation
All things are in decay.

For Man is ev'ry thing,
And more: He is a tree, yet bears more fruit;
A beast, yet is, or should be more:
10   Reason and speech we onely bring.
Parrats may thank us, if they are not mute,
They go upon the score.

Man is all symmetrie,
Full of proportions, one limbe to another,
15   And all to all the world besides:
Each part may call the furthest, brother:
For head with foot hath private amitie,
And both with moons and tides.

Nothing hath got so farre,
20   But Man hath caught and kept it, as his prey.
His eyes dismount the highest starre:
He is in little all the sphere.
Herbs gladly cure our flesh; because that they
Finde their acquaintance there.

25   For us the windes do blow,
The earth doth rest, heav'n move, and fountains flow.
Nothing we see, but means our good,
As our delight, or as our treasure:
The whole is, either our cupboard of food,
30   Or cabinet of pleasure.

The starres have us to bed;
Night draws the curtain, which the sunne withdraws;
Musick and light attend our head.
All things unto our flesh are kinde

35 In their descent and being; to our minde
        In their ascent and cause.

        Each thing is full of dutie:
    Waters united are our navigation;
       Distinguished, our habitation;
40   Below, our drink; above, our meat;
    Both are our cleanlinesse. Hath one such beautie?
       Then how are all things neat?

       More servants wait on Man,
    Than he'l take notice of: in ev'ry path
45   He treads down that which doth befriend him,
       When sicknesse makes him pale and wan.
  Oh mightie love! Man is one world, and hath
       Another to attend him.

       Since then, my God, thou hast
50 So brave a Palace built; O dwell in it,
       That it may dwell with thee at last!
       Till then, afford us so much wit;
  That, as the world serves us, we may serve thee,
       And both thy servants be.

1 *I heard this day:* Hutchinson suggests that although both Herbert and Vaughan employ the "casual and almost colloquial allusion to a day in the first line of a poem, e.g. *Affliction V*, 'My God, I read this day', and Vaughan's 'I saw Eternity the other night' and 'I walkt the other day (to spend my hour)' ", Herbert may possibly have heard the reading of the lesson or a sermon preached on *Luke*, xiv, 28–30.

2 *a stately habitation:* cf. Herbert's "The World", l. 1: "Love built a stately house."

5 *then . . . to:* than; compared to.

7–8 *For Man . . . And more:* This statement goes beyond the notion, still common in Herbert's day (cf. "The Good-morrow", l. 14, and "The Exequy", l. 55), of man as the microcosm, the "little world" that Herbert again refers to in ll. 22 and 47 here. The argument that man is even more than "ev'ry thing" recalls Donne, *XXVI Sermons*, xxv, 370: "The properties, the qualities of every Creature, are in man; the Essence, the Existence of every Creature is for man; so man is every Creature. And therefore the

Philosopher draws man into too narrow a table, when he says he is *Micro-cosmos*, an Abridgement of the world in little: *Nazianzen* gives him but his due, when he calls him *Mundum Magnum*, a world to which all the rest of the world is but subordinate."

8 *yet bears more fruit:* in the very variety of his virtues and achievements.

11–12 *Parrats . . . the score:* i.e. Parrots, if they can speak, owe it to man and this too is scored to his credit.

14–18 *Full of proportions . . . tides:* i.e. Each part of the human body is in perfect proportion to its fellows and also to all the rest of the world. The motions of stars and planets, moon and tides, were thought to influence different parts of the body—microcosm working in a relation of harmonious "amitie" with the surrounding macrocosm in an ordered organic whole. Cf. l. 16 with ll. 5–6 of Herbert's poem "Dooms-day": "While this member jogs the other,/Each one whispring, *Live you brother?*" Cf. also Traherne, "The Salutation", ll. 21–4.

21 *His eyes . . . starre:* Cf. a similar tribute to the superior power of man's sight over the rest of creation in Donne's "The Sunne Rising", l. 13, in which the lover can eclipse the rays of the sun merely by closing his eyes.

23–4 *because . . . acquaintance there:* i.e. because they recognize in his flesh the affinity with their own (cf. *Isaiah* xl, 6–7: "All flesh is grass, and all the goodliness thereof is as the flower of the field: The grass withereth, the flower fadeth"). Also perhaps because in serving man they find fulfilment of their function in the universe (with "acquaintance" used in the sense of "proper purpose" as well as "kinship and correspondence").

34–6 *All things . . . cause:* i.e. All things minister to the body in their coming down from God, their nature and their existence; to the mind, in leading it up to their origin.

37 *dutie:* usefulness and service to us.

39 *Distinguished:* separated from the land (*Genesis* i, 9–10) to provide a habitation for man.

40 *Below . . . meat:* i.e. on earth, our drink; falling from above as rain, the provider of food.

41–2 *Hath one . . . neat?:* i.e. If one element alone has such a beauty and variety of use, then how much more must the whole creation be fit and appropriately framed ("neat") to serve us?

44–6 *in ev'ry path . . . wan:* Cf. ll. 23–4, and Donne *XXVI Sermons*, viii, 111: "we tread upon many herbs negligently in the field, but when we see them in an Apothecaries shop, we begin to think that there is some vertue in them."

50–1 *So brave . . . last!:* a return to the opening image of the "stately habitation", with a play on the idea of "dwelling" in the plea that God may inhabit the human "Palace" on earth in order to fit man to live ultimately with him in heaven.

53-4 *That . . . servants be:* Here again is Herbert's recurring image of service (see footnote to l. 16 of "Love", p. 105): of the world's service to man and of man's, by analogy and in gratitude, to God, thus making them both his servants.

REDEMPTION

THIS sonnet offers a vivid reflection and reminder of Herbert's work as a country parson. He dramatizes the story of his search, culminating in Christ's redemption of man on the Cross, with the narrative and pictorial directness he might have used in relating it from the pulpit to his country congregations, translating it into the terms—tenant and landlord, lease and land-purchase—closest to their own recognizable everyday experience. The metaphor of the legal transaction recalls Ralegh's imagery of court and lawyers in ll. 35-50 of "The Passionate Mans Pilgrimage" (pp. 77-8); and it is interesting to compare "Redemption" with the legal terms Donne also employs in his Holy Sonnet XVI ("Father, part of his double interest"). Herbert sustains the conceit right through to his laconic conclusion, where the spelling of the final words, "& died", imitates the phraseology of the legal document. Joan Bennett in *Five Metaphysical Poets* likens the plain matter-of-factness of Herbert's narration to "the tone of men exchanging news in the market place", and Eliot uses the poem to illustrate his observation that "Herbert is a master of the simple everyday word in the right place, and charges it with concentrated meaning". In its powerful and poignant simplicity the sonnet makes its point with the economy, precision and impact of any New Testament parable.

> Having been tenant long to a rich Lord,
>   Not thriving, I resolved to be bold,
>   And make a suit unto him, to afford
> A new small-rented lease, and cancell th' old.
> 5   In heaven at his manour I him sought:
>   They told me there, that he was lately gone
>   About some land, which he had dearly bought
>   Long since on earth, to take possession.

I straight return'd, and knowing his great birth,
10   Sought him accordingly in great resorts;
In cities, theatres, gardens, parks, and courts:
At length I heard a ragged noise and mirth
Of theeves and murderers: there I him espied,
Who straight, *Your suit is granted*, said, & died.

3 *suit:* petition. The idea of the suitor is echoed in "The Collar", ll. 6 and 31.

12 *ragged:* rough. "The phrase 'ragged noise and mirth'," says Eliot, "gives us, in four words, the picture of the scene to which Herbert wishes to introduce us."

LOVE (III)

ELIOT finds it significant that this third poem of Herbert's entitled "Love" should be the last in his volume *The Temple*, as an indication of his ultimate acceptance of God's grace and mercy beyond all rebellions, and of "the serenity finally attained by this proud and humble man". Like "Redemption" it is couched in the form of a parable: that of guest and host, the one travel-stained and diffident, the other graciously welcoming, taking a meal together. Implicit in the image is the communion table of the altar, the "board" as rudely flouted at the opening of "The Collar" as it is now courteously accepted. There is a moving simplicity in the language, and by the end, as Joan Bennett remarks, "the emotion has become so poignant that the simple monosyllables 'So I did sit and eat' convey more than the most impassioned rhetoric".

Love bade me welcome: yet my soul drew back,
      Guiltie of dust and sinne.
But quick-ey'd Love, observing me grow slack
      From my first entrance in,
5 Drew nearer to me, sweetly questioning,
      If I lack'd any thing.

A guest, I answer'd, worthy to be here:
      Love said, You shall be he.

I the unkinde, ungratefull? Ah my deare,
10   I cannot look on thee.
Love took my hand, and smiling did reply,
     Who made the eyes but I?

Truth Lord, but I have marr'd them: let my shame
     Go where it doth deserve.
15 And know you not, sayes Love, who bore the blame?
     My deare, then I will serve.
You must sit downe, sayes Love, and taste my meat:
     So I did sit and eat.

9 *Ah my deare:* Cf. the identical use of this phrase of affection addressed to Christ in Gerard Manley Hopkins's "The Windhover", l. 12.

16 *serve:* The idea of service constantly recurs in Herbert's relation with God (cf. "Affliction", ll. 2, 13 and 63, "The Collar", l. 31, and "Man", ll. 53–4).

Henry Vaughan

THE WORLD

MANY of the poems of Henry Vaughan (1621/2–95) are based on scriptural texts. Here it is I *John* ii, 16, 17: "All that is in the world, the lust of the flesh, the lust of the Eyes, and the pride of life, is not of the Father, but is of the world. And the world passeth away, and the lusts thereof, but he that doth the will of God abideth for ever." The central antithesis opposes light and darkness, God and the world; the calm and brightness of eternity with the restless and fruitless activity of men moving in time, its shadow. Throughout his work Vaughan's most memorable passages employ images of light as the symbol of spiritual illumination. Profoundly influenced by Herbert, "the blessed man"—as Vaughan called him in the Preface to the enlarged edition of his *Silex Scintillans*, 1655—"whose holy *life* and *verse* gained many pious *Converts*, (of whom I am the least)", Vaughan borrowed freely from the themes and titles, images and metres, of *The Temple*. He lacks Herbert's sense of form, discipline and economy of language, and his ability to sustain the same poetic level throughout a poem. Yet at his best, in moments of intense spiritual exaltation—as in the celebrated opening of this poem—Vaughan "sees *Invisibles*" (his own phrase) with a soaring lyrical and mystical rapture outside Herbert's compass.

> I saw Eternity the other night
> Like a great *Ring* of pure and endless light,
>   All calm, as it was bright,
> And round beneath it, Time in hours, days, years
> 5   Driv'n by the spheres
> Like a vast shadow mov'd, In which the world
>   And all her train were hurl'd;

The doting Lover in his queintest strain
      Did there Complain,
10 Neer him, his Lute, his fancy, and his flights,
      Wits sour delights,
With gloves, and knots the silly snares of pleasure
      Yet his dear Treasure
All scatter'd lay, while he his eys did pour
15   Upon a flowr.

The darksome States-man hung with weights and woe
Like a thick midnight-fog mov'd there so slow
      He did nor stay, nor go;
Condemning thoughts (like sad Ecclipses) scowl
20   Upon his soul,
And Clouds of crying witnesses without
      Pursued him with one shout.
Yet dig'd the Mole, and lest his ways be found
      Workt under ground,
25 Where he did Clutch his prey, but one did see
      That policie,
Churches and altars fed him, Perjuries
      Were gnats and flies,
It rain'd about him bloud and tears, but he
30   Drank them as free.

The fearfull miser on a heap of rust
Sate pining all his life there, did scarce trust
      His own hands with the dust,
Yet would not place one peece above, but lives
35   In feare of theeves.
Thousands there were as frantick as himself
      And hug'd each one his pelf,
The down-right Epicure plac'd heav'n in sense
      And scornd pretence
40 While others slipt into a wide Excesse
      Said little lesse;
The weaker sort slight, triviall wares Inslave
      Who think them brave,

And poor, despised truth sate Counting by
45   Their victory.

Yet some, who all this while did weep and sing,
And sing, and weep, soar'd up into the *Ring*,
      But most would use no wing.
O fools (said I,) thus to prefer dark night
50   Before true light,
To live in grots, and caves, and hate the day
      Because it shews the way,
The way which from this dead and dark abode
      Leads up to God,
55 A way where you might tread the Sun, and be
      More bright than he.
But as I did their madnes so discusse
      One whisper'd thus,
This Ring the Bride-groome did for none provide
60   *But for his bride.*

2 *Like a great* Ring: Owen Felltham, a poet Vaughan admired and one of the influences on his early secular poetry, wrote in *Resolves*, i, 9, "Of Time's continuall speede", of Virtue and Vice travelling through the world with their attendants and contending for man's soul: "And behinde all these, came *Eternity*, casting a *Ring* about them, which like a strong *inchantment*, made them for ever the same." Vaughan also uses the image of the ring in a similar sense in "To Amoret, Walking in a Starry Evening" (l. 7) and in "Vanity of Spirit" (ll. 5–6).

5 *Driv'n by the spheres:* In Ptolemaic astronomy the sun was believed to move on one of a system of concentric spheres, of which the earth was the centre. The moon and the other heavenly bodies also had their spheres. Time is turned by the movement of the spheres into the shadow of eternity's ring of light.

7 *her train:* following of ephemeral lusts.

8–12 *The doting Lover . . . pleasure:* Cf. Herbert, "Dulnesse", l. 5: "The wanton lover in a curious strain". After his conversion Vaughan, like Donne, dissociated himself from his earlier secular poetry and the poets he had imitated ("those ingenious persons, which in the late Notion are termed Wits"). The allusion to "Wits sour delights" expresses his new revulsion from profane love poetry; and the trivial preoccupations of the "doting

Lover" stand in implicit contrast with the true and lasting Love of ll. 59–60.

13–15 *Yet . . . flowr:* i.e. His eyes are turned not towards his true treasure, but fixed upon a temporal and transitory object.

16–24 *The darksome States-man . . . under ground:* The contrast with the ring of light is most intense in these emotive images and atmosphere of darkness ("darksome", "thick midnight-fog", "sad Ecclipses", "Clouds") which conjure the activity of the politician in his lust for power, condemned by all in thought and word and compared in his deviousness with the underground workings of the mole. Cf. Herbert, "Confession", ll. 14–15: "Like moles within us, heave, and cast about:/And till they foot and clutch their prey . . ."

25–6 *one . . . policie:* i.e. Despite his cunning his policy does not deceive.

27–30 *Churches . . . free:* i.e. He thrives alike on the church and on lies and broken promises, and freely drinks the blood and tears caused by his actions.

31–5 *The fearfull miser . . . theeves:* cf. *Matthew* vi, 19–21. The miser pines his life away in apprehension of being robbed of his worthless hoard, scarcely trusting himself with it yet refusing to lay up even one piece of treasure in heaven.

38–9 *plac'd heav'n . . . pretence:* i.e. frankly admitted that he found heaven in sensual satisfaction.

42–3 *The weaker sort . . . brave:* i.e. Weaker men, less bold in their excesses, prize the trivial and think it handsome ("brave").

44–5 *And poor . . . victory:* Cf. Herbert, "The Church Militant": "While Truth sat by, counting his victories". But here neglected truth counts not his own but the victory of the enemy forces which tempt men from him.

48 *would use no wing:* would make no effort to soar in spirit.

57–60 *But . . . bride:* Cf. the intervention of the supernatural Voice at the end of "The Collar" (p. 93). The opening image of the ring as a circle of light now takes on a second meaning with the introduction of the Bridegroom, Christ, and his mystical marriage with the soul, his bride (cf. Vaughan's "The Queer", ll. 3–4: "Which wears heaven, like a bridal ring,/And tramples on doubts and despair?").

THE NIGHT

THIS poem also springs from a biblical epigraph (*John* iii, 2: "The same came to Jesus by night, and said unto him, Rabbi, we know that thou art a teacher come from God: for no man can do these miracles that thou doest, except God be with him"), and contains many allusions to other scriptural texts. It is interesting to compare and contrast with "The World", where earthly pleasures and preoccupations are embodied in the central image of darkness, and God and eternity in that of light. Here it is not in the activity of "busie fools" in "this worlds ill-guiding light" that God is to be sought and found, but in the darkness and silence of night, "this worlds defeat . . . cares check and curb", the "souls calm retreat". Cf. Vaughan's *The Mount of Olives*, in which he speaks of the night as the "*portion* of time . . . of all others the most powerful to excite thee to *devotion*".

> Through that pure *Virgin-shrine*,
> That sacred vail drawn o'r thy glorious noon
> That men might look and live as Glo-worms shine,
>   And face the Moon:
> 5   Wise *Nicodemus* saw such light
> As made him know his God by night.
>
> Most blest believer he!
> Who in that land of darkness and blinde eyes
> Thy long expected healing wings could see,
> 10   When thou didst rise,
> And what can never more be done,
> Did at mid-night speak with the Sun!
>
> O who will tell me, where
> He found thee at that dead and silent hour!
> 15   What hallow'd solitary ground did bear
>   So rare a flower,
> Within whose sacred leafs did lie
> The fulness of the Deity.
>
> No mercy-seat of gold,
> 20   No dead and dusty *Cherub*, nor carv'd stone,
> But his own living works did my Lord hold
>   And lodge alone;
> Where *trees* and *herbs* did watch and peep
> And wonder, while the *Jews* did sleep.

25   Dear night! this worlds defeat;
The stop to busie fools; cares check and curb;
The day of Spirits; my souls calm retreat
     Which none disturb!
Christs progress, and his prayer time;
30   The hours to which high Heaven doth chime.

     Gods silent, searching flight:
When my Lords head is fill'd with dew, and all
His locks are wet with the clear drops of night;
     His still, soft call;
35   His knocking time; The souls dumb watch,
When Spirits their fair kindred catch.

     Were all my loud, evil days
Calm and unhaunted as is thy dark Tent,
Whose peace but by some *Angels* wing or voice
40   Is seldom rent;
Then I in Heaven all the long year
Would keep, and never wander here.

     But living where the Sun
Doth all things wake, and where all mix and tyre
45 Themselves and others, I consent and run
     To ev'ry myre,
And by this worlds ill-guiding light,
Erre more than I can do by night.

     There is in God (some say)
50 A deep, but dazling darkness; As men here
Say it is late and dusky, because they
     See not all clear
O for that night! where I in him
Might live invisible and dim.

---

5 *Wise* Nicodemus: A Pharisee, Nicodemus was a secret disciple of Christ.
9–12 *Thy long expected . . . Sun!:* Cf. *Malachi* iv, 2: "But unto you that
fear my name shall the Sun of righteousness arise with healing in his wings."
19–24 *No mercy-seat . . . sleep:* i.e. Christ is not contained in the golden

glories, cherubim and rich carvings described in the building of Solomon's temple (II *Chronicles* iii and iv), but in "his own living works" of "*trees and herbs*" ("my Lord" is the direct object of "hold" and "lodge"). Cf. *Luke* xxi, 37: "And in the day time he was teaching in the temple; and at night he went out, and abode in the mount that is called the mount of Olives."

27 *The day of Spirits:* i.e. Because the night is a refuge from worldly business and cares, it is like day for the spirit. Cf. Vaughan's *Of Life and Death*: "the watching of the body is the sleep of the Soul . . . the day was made for Corporeall Actions, but the night is the working-time of Spirits."

29 *Christs progress . . . time:* cf. *Mark* i, 35: "And in the morning rising up a great while before day, he went out, and departed into a solitary place, and there prayed."

32–5 *When my Lords head . . . knocking time:* cf. *Song of Solomon*, v, 2: "I sleep, but my heart waketh: it is the voice of my beloved that knocketh, saying, Open to me, my sister, my love, my dove, my undefiled: for my head is filled with dew, and my locks with the drops of the night." Cf. also *Revelation*, iii, 20: "Behold, I stand at the door, and knock."

39 *but:* except.

42 *keep:* live, remain.

44 *mix:* confuse.

46 *myre:* swamp of sin.

49–54 *There is . . . dim:* Like the opening of "The World", this is one of those passages of mystical ecstasy which assure Vaughan his high place among the English religious poets. The paradox of "dazling darkness" superbly conveys that inner illumination enabled only by the silence and calm of night. Note the effectiveness of the alliteration in ll. 50–1 and of the assonance in ll. 53–4.

MAN

IT is interesting to contrast Vaughan's view of man with Herbert's in his poem of the same title (p. 99). For Herbert, man is the superior form of life on earth, to whom all elements and creatures are subordinate and subservient: compared with his creation, "All things are in decay". Vaughan, on the other hand, sees the human creature alone falling short of the "stedfastness" to be observed in lesser, "mean things" such as birds, bees and flowers. Their ordered habits and obedience to God's law rebuke by com-

parison the irregular, restless motions of man as he "About the earth doth
run and ride", bewildered and lost, knowing neither where he is going nor
what his spirit craves. Where Herbert envisages man at home in a world
where "The whole is, either our cupboard of food,/Or cabinet of pleasure",
Vaughan perceives only a rootless exile, driven to feverish activity in vain
quest of the true home he has long since forgotten. Reiterating his con-
demnation in "The World" of the futility of men's trivial pursuits, and in
"The Night" of the activity of "busie fools" in "this worlds ill-guiding
light", Vaughan once more communicates in this poem his frequent sense
of man as a stranger and a prisoner on earth, the one jarring note in the
universal harmony of existence. His conclusion strongly echoes Herbert's
theme in "The Pulley". Yet even here Vaughan withholds the satisfaction
afforded by Herbert in providing a good reason for God's ordinance in
denying man rest, so that he is made to seem a mere helpless and pointless
victim of his own nature.

      Weighing the stedfastness and state
    Of some mean things which here below reside,
   Where birds like watchful Clocks the noiseless date
       And Intercourse of times divide,
5   Where Bees at night get home and hive, and flowrs
        Early, as well as late,
   Rise with the Sun, and set in the same bowrs;

      I would (said I) my God would give
    The staidness of these things to man! for these
10 To his divine appointments ever cleave,
       And no new business breaks their peace;
   The birds nor sow, nor reap, yet sup and dine,
       The flowres without clothes live,
   Yet *Solomon* was never drest so fine.

15   Man hath still either toyes, or Care,
    He hath no root, nor to one place is ty'd,
   But ever restless and Irregular
       About this Earth doth run and ride,
   He knows he hath a home, but scarce knows where,
20   He sayes it is so far
   That he hath quite forgot how to go there.

He knocks at all doors, strays and roams,
Nay hath not so much wit as some stones have
Which in the darkest nights point to their homes,
25   By some hid sense their Maker gave;
Man is the shuttle, to whose winding quest
And passage through these looms
God order'd motion, but ordain'd no rest.

1 *stedfastness and state:* constancy and condition of life.

5 *Where Bees . . . hive:* Cf. Herbert, "The Starre", ll. 30–1: "To flie home like a laden bee/Unto that hive of beams".

9 *staidness:* steadiness, stability.

12–14 *The birds . . . so fine:* Cf. *Matthew* vi, 26, 28–9.

15 *still . . . Care:* always either trivial pleasures and amusements or worldly worries.

19–21 *He knows . . . go there:* by contrast with "The Retreate", where man in his infancy does still know where his home is; as also in "Corruption", ll. 5–6 and 19–20:

He saw Heaven o'er his head, and knew from whence
He came (condemned,) hither . . .
He sigh'd for *Eden*, and would often say
Ah! what bright days were those?

23–5 *Nay . . . gave:* i.e. He has not so much sense as loadstones (a variety of natural iron oxide which exerts a magnetic attraction). Traherne too uses a loadstone image in *Centuries I*, 2: "Things unknown have a Secret Influence on the Soul: and like the Centre of the Earth unseen, violently Attract it. We lov we know not what: and therfore evry Thing allures us. As Iron at a Distance is drawn by the Loadstone, there being some Invisible Communications between them: So is there in us a World of Lov to somwhat, tho we know not what in the World that should be."

26–8 *Man . . . rest:* This image of the shuttle winding incessantly through the looms of life is peculiarly apt for the restless activity of man on earth.

THE MORNING-WATCH

THE central idea of this poem—of prayer as "the world in tune"—may have been suggested by a line of Herbert's in "Prayer (I)" in which he likens it to

"A kind of tune, which all things heare and fear". Vaughan's four opening
words also recall Herbert in another poem, "The Holy Scriptures (I)":
"Oh Book! infinite sweetnesse!" "The Morning-watch" couples nature's
joy in the return of light with that of his soul waking from sleep as it will
also (by implication at the end) from death; and Joan Bennett calls it "perhaps the most perfect whole among all Vaughan's poems". The mounting
ecstatic surge of praise, coming finally to rest on a quieter note of calm
certitude, is beautifully controlled and communicated through the movement of a metre which echoes the ebb and flow of the feeling.

> O Joyes! Infinite sweetnes! with what flowres,
> And shoots of glory, my soul breakes, and buds!
>   All the long houres
>   Of night, and Rest
> 5   Through the still shrouds
>   Of sleep, and Clouds,
>   This Dew fell on my Breast;
>   O how it *Blouds*,
> And *Spirits* all my Earth! heark! In what Rings,
> 10 And *Hymning Circulations* the quick world
>   Awakes, and sings;
>   The rising winds,
>   And falling springs,
>   Birds, beasts, all things
> 15   Adore him in their kinds.
>   Thus all is hurl'd
> In sacred *Hymnes*, and *Order*, The great *Chime*
> And *Symphony* of nature. Prayer is
>   The world in tune,
> 20   A spirit-voyce,
>   And vocall joyes
>   Whose *Eccho is* heav'ns blisse.
>   O let me climbe
> When I lye down! The Pious soul by night
> 25 Is like a clouded starre, whose beames though sed
>   To shed their light
>   Under some Cloud
>   Yet are above,

                           And shine, and move
30   Beyond that mistie shrowd.
                           So in my Bed
            That Curtain'd grave, though sleep, like ashes, hide
            My lamp, and life, both shall in thee abide.

1-2 *with what flowres . . . buds!:* Cf. "The Retreate", l. 20 and footnote
(pp. 120-1).

3-7 *All . . . Breast:* Cf. the central notion of "The Night", that these
"long houres" of stillness and darkness are the time of spiritual renewal,
the "souls calm retreat". The "Dew" of grace echoes the image of ll. 32-3
of "The Night".

8-10 *O how it* Blouds . . . Hymning Circulations: Burton's *Anatomy*
describes the belief that from the blood "*Spirits* are first begotten in the heart,
which afterwards by the arteries are communicated to the other parts".
(See footnote to "The Exstasie", ll. 61-7, p. 28.) Joan Bennett observes that
"Vaughan combines the old and new physiology. . . . William Harvey's
discovery of the circulation of the blood was published in 1628. Vaughan,
himself a physician, would presumably have been interested. In these lines
both the blood-begotten vital spirits and the circular movement of the blood
represent the revitalizing of the poet and of the rest of the created world,
at dawn. Vaughan often italicizes words to which he wants to draw the
reader's attention, but no critic, as far as I know, has especially attended to
the relation between *Blouds-Spirits-Hymning Circulations*" (*Five Metaphysical
Poets*).

9 *Rings:* Cf. the figure of the "*Ring*", in a different meaning, in l. 2
of "The World" (and footnote).

10 *quick:* alive, sentient.

15 *in their kinds:* according to their own natures and ways.

16 *hurl'd:* As in l. 7 of "The World", the verb communicates a sense of
powerful movement.

23-4 *O let me climbe . . . down!:* a typical metaphysical paradox. Cf.
Donne's "Hymne to God my God, in my sicknesse", l. 30.

27 *Cloud:* Cf. l. 6.

31-2 *So in my Bed . . . grave:* This analogy of sleep with death, continuing
the suggestion of "shrouds" in ll. 5 and 30, recalls Donne's in "Death be
not proud", l. 5.

"THEY ARE ALL GONE INTO THE WORLD OF LIGHT!"

THIS untitled meditation on death, with its bereft sadness in the first and third verses, was perhaps prompted by the death in 1648 of Vaughan's much-loved younger brother William and that of his first wife Catherine, who died in or about 1653, two years before the publication of the second part of *Silex Scintillans* in which this poem was included. Yet it is, paradoxically, one of Vaughan's poems most steadily pervaded by the sense of light which for him is synonymous with the world of spirit. His use of the verbs "glow", "glitter", "glimmer", and "burn", the images of stars, of the "Air of glory" in which the dead walk "whose light doth trample on my days", and of death as a jewel which shines in the darkness of life, combine to illumine the whole poem with a visionary radiance.

> They are all gone into the world of light!
>   And I alone sit lingring here;
> Their very memory is fair and bright,
>   And my sad thoughts doth clear.
>
> 5   It glows and glitters in my cloudy brest
>   Like stars upon some gloomy grove,
> Or those faint beams in which this hill is drest,
>   After the Sun's remove.
>
> I see them walking in an Air of glory,
> 10   Whose light doth trample on my days:
> My days, which are at best but dull and hoary,
>   Meer glimering and decays.
>
> O holy hope! and high humility,
>   High as the Heavens above!
> 15 These are your walks, and you have shew'd them me
>   To kindle my cold love,
>
> Dear, beauteous death! the Jewel of the Just,
>   Shining no where, but in the dark;

What mysteries do lie beyond thy dust;
20   Could man outlook that mark!

He that hath found some fledg'd birds nest, may know
  At first sight, if the bird be flown;
But what fair Well, or Grove he sings in now,
  That is to him unknown.

25 And yet, as Angels in some brighter dreams
  Call to the soul, when man doth sleep:
So some strange thoughts transcend our wonted theams,
  And into glory peep.

If a star were confin'd into a Tomb
30   Her captive flames must needs burn there;
But when the hand that lockt her up, gives room,
  She'l shine through all the sphære.

O Father of eternal life, and all
  Created glories under thee!
35 Resume thy spirit from this world of thrall
  Into true liberty.

Either disperse these mists, which blot and fill
  My perspective (still) as they pass,
Or else remove me hence unto that hill,
40   Where I shall need no glass.

17 *the Jewel of the Just:* i.e. because of their rebirth into immortality which lies beyond it.

25–6 *And yet . . . sleep:* Cf. Donne's "Aire and Angels", ll. 3–4, and see also headnote to the poem (p. 21) and note to l. 2 of "The Retreate".

29–32 *If a star . . . sphære:* The analogy is between the star and the spirit of the dead. Cf. Vaughan's "The Bird", ll. 19–20: "For each inclosed Spirit is a star/Inlightning his own little sphære."

33–6 *O Father . . . true liberty:* Cf. *Romans* viii, 21: "Because the creature itself also shall be delivered from the bondage of corruption into the glorious liberty of the children of God."

35 *resume:* take back, recover.

37 *these mists:* i.e. which hide truth from the finite vision of man on earth.

38 *perspective:* spy-glass, telescope.
40 *glass:* i.e. the telescope.

THE RETREATE

VAUGHAN regarded with especial reverence the early years of life before
the human spirit is separated from its source: that "first, happy age;/An
age without distast and warrs" ("Looking Back"), the "dear, harmless age!
the short, swift span,/Where weeping virtue parts with man" ("Childe-
hood"). With a tautness and concentration lacking in much of his work,
he expresses in the following poem a conviction derived equally from the
Platonic doctrine of the soul's pre-existence and the Christian idea of the
child's innocence (*Mark* x, 14–15). His yearning to regain that lost clarity
and purity of vision echoes his lament in "Childe-hood": "I cannot reach
it; and my striving eye/Dazzles at it, as at eternity." Vaughan may have
read John Earle's "Character of a Child" (*Micro-cosmographie*, 1628): "*A
Child* is . . . the best Copie of *Adam* before hee tasted of *Eve*, or the Apple . . .
Hee is natures fresh picture newly drawne in Oyle, which time and much
handling dimmes and defaces . . . The elder he growes, he is a stayre lower
from God." (Vaughan also repeats the last thought in "Distraction": "I find
my selfe the lesse, the more I grow.") The affinities have often been noted
between this poem and Wordsworth's "Ode on the Intimations of Immortality":

> But trailing clouds of glory do we come
>   From God, who is our home:
> Heaven lies about us in our infancy!

Happy those early dayes! when I
Shin'd in my Angell-infancy.
Before I understood this place
Appointed for my second race,
5   Or taught my soul to fancy ought
But a white, Celestiall thought,
When yet I had not walkt above
A mile, or two, from my first love,
And looking back (at that short space,)
10   Could see a glimpse of his bright-face;

When on some *gilded Cloud,* or *flowre*
My gazing soul would dwell an houre,
And in those weaker glories spy
Some shadows of eternity;
15 Before I taught my tongue to wound
My Conscience with a sinfull sound,
Or had the black art to dispence
A sev'rall sinne to ev'ry sence,
But felt through all this fleshly dresse
20 Bright *shootes* of *everlastingnesse*
O how I long to travell back
And tread again that ancient track!
That I might once more reach that plaine,
Where first I left my glorious traine,
25 From whence th' Inlightned spirit sees
That shady City of Palme trees;
But (ah!) my soul with too much stay
Is drunk, and staggers in the way.
Some men a forward motion love,
30 But I by backward steps would move,
And when this dust falls to the urn
In that state I came return.

---

2 *Angell-infancy:* an association with Vaughan's frequent idea (shared by Blake) of angels inhabiting the world as man's familiars.

4 *my second race:* His first was the existence which preceded his being born into this world.

5 *ought:* anything.

8 *my first love:* This phrase (or "early love") recurs in various other poems of Vaughan's to express man's relation with God. Cf. also *Revelation* ii, 4: ". . . thou hast left thy first love".

11–14 *When . . . eternity:* In all Vaughan's poetry the "weaker glories" of Nature are seen as the visible proof and pledge of God, whose "glory through the world dost drive". Cf. the idea of temporal objects as "shadows" of eternity in l. 6 of "The World".

17 *black art:* sorcerer's magic, in contrast with the "white, Celestiall thought" (l. 6). Brightness (l. 10) and whiteness again symbolize holiness, and darkness, sin.

20 shootes *of everlastingnesse:* One of Vaughan's favourite images for the soul is that of a flower or plant, and buds and shoots occur in various poems. Also cf. Felltham (see note on ll. 1–7 of "The World"), *Resolves,* i, 64, "Of the Soule": "The *Conscience,* the *Caracter* of a *God* stampt in it, and the apprehension of *Eternity,* doe all prove it a *shoot of everlastingnesse.*"

26 *City of Palme trees:* an echo of the phrase in *Deuteronomy* xxxiv, 3, describing Jericho.

27 *stay:* dwelling in this world.

29–32 *Some men . . . return:* As the shining, brightness and whiteness of purity and eternity are opposed to the blackness of sin, the shadow of time, so the polarities of backward and forward conclude the poem with a paradox: he can go backward, and return to the child's state of mind, heart and spirit towards which he aspires, only by the "forward motion" of his body in its physical progress towards death, when his soul will be restored to its original innocence.

Thomas Traherne

THE SALUTATION

STRIKING similarities in style and in their attitude towards childhood—
"The first Impressions are Immortall all," declared Traherne—caused the
poems of Thomas Traherne (1637/8–74) to be at first attributed to Vaughan.
None was published in his lifetime, nor were the manuscripts discovered
until over two centuries later. A first volume was published in 1903 and a
second, prepared after his early death with revisions by his brother Philip,
under the title of *Poems of Felicity*, in 1910. Traherne's perception of the
kinship between the fresh "Infant-Ey" view of the universe and the mystic's
intuitions of harmony and happiness often recalls not only Vaughan but
Blake and Wordsworth. But whereas Vaughan in "The Retreate" mourns a
purer pre-existence the child has left behind, Traherne in this poem sees his
soul as well as his body as having been "Nothing from Eternitie", and now
awakening to rejoice in his inherited wealth, "this Glorious Store . . . this
fair World". The "Strange Glories" he experiences through his attainment
of human form are infused by the philosophy of dedicated joy which
Traherne described as "Christian epicureanism". His celebration of the
gift of existence, the intricate mechanism of the body "In which a Soul doth
Dwell", and the diversity of its "Sacred Treasures" which he separately
savours, embodies his profound conviction of the interdependence of the
worlds of sense and spirit, each enriching and intensifying the other.

> These little Limmes,
> These Eys and Hands which here I find,
> These rosie Cheeks wherwith my Life begins,
> Where have ye been? Behind
> 5 What Curtain were ye from me hid so long!
> Where was? in what Abyss, my Speaking Tongue?

When silent I,
So many thousand thousand yeers,
Beneath the Dust did in a Chaos lie,
10   How could I Smiles or Tears,
Or Lips or Hands or Eys or Ears perceiv?
Welcom ye Treasures which I now receiv.

I that so long
Was Nothing from Eternitie,
15 Did little think such Joys as Ear or Tongue,
        To Celebrat or See:
Such Sounds to hear, such Hands to feel, such Feet,
Beneath the Skies, on such a Ground to meet.

New Burnisht Joys!
20   Which yellow Gold and Pearl excell!
Such Sacred Treasures are the Lims in Boys,
       In which a Soul doth Dwell;
Their Organized Joynts, and Azure Veins
More Wealth include, then all the World contains.

25   From Dust I rise,
    And out of Nothing now awake,
These Brighter Regions which salute mine Eys,
      A Gift from GOD I take.
The Earth, the Seas, the Light, the Day, the Skies,
30 The Sun and Stars are mine; if those I prize.

Long time before
I in my Mothers Womb was born,
A GOD preparing did this Glorious Store,
      The World for me adorne.
35 Into this Eden so Divine and fair,
So Wide and Bright, I com his Son and Heir.

A Stranger here
Strange Things doth meet, Strange Glories See;
Strange Treasures lodg'd in this fair World appear,
40   Strange all, and New to me.

But that they mine should be, who nothing was,
That Strangest is of all, yet brought to pass.

9 *the Dust:* out of which man was created (*Genesis*); as also in l. 25.

29–30 *The Earth . . . prize:* Traherne often turns into verse, using similar
or identical phraseology, some idea expressed in his prose. Cf. *Centuries of
Meditations I*, 29: "You never Enjoy the World aright, till the Sea it self
floweth in your Veins, till you are Clothed with the Heavens, and Crowned
with the Stars"; and 35: "The Riches of the Light are the Works of God,
which are the Portion and Inheritance of his sons, to be seen and enjoyed
in Heaven and Earth, the Sea, and all that is therin, the Light and the Day."

35 *Into this Eden . . . fair:* Cf. "Eden", ll. 36–8: "Those Things which first
his Eden did adorn,/My Infancy/Did crown."

36 *his Son and Heir:* Cf. *Centuries I*, 29: "and Perceiv your self to be the
Sole Heir of the whole World."

37–42 *A Stranger here . . . to pass:* Cf. *Centuries III*, 2: "All appeared New,
and Strange at the first, inexpressibly rare, and Delightfull, and Beautifull.
I was a little Stranger which at my Enterance into the World was Saluted
and Surrounded with innumerable Joys."

ON NEWS

THIS is the version of the poem which appears as No. 26 in *Centuries of
Meditations III*, following the passages beginning "When I heard of any
New Kingdom beyond the seas, the Light and Glory of it pleased me im-
mediatly, enterd into me, it rose up within me and I was Enlarged Wonder-
fully" (24), and "When I heard any News I received it with Greediness and
Delight, becaus my Expectation was awakend with som Hope that My
Happiness and the Thing I wanted was concealed in it" (25). Traherne
describes here the child's intimations of a world whose now "Absent Bliss"
beckons him to its rediscovery, with his senses acting as ambassadors which
bring news from the place which houses his true wealth. The ear, in stanza
1, communicates the "Joyfull Tidings" to the soul, which waits like a
host on the threshold of sense, its "dwelling place", and would almost leave
it in eagerness to go out and entertain its guest, "the Unknown Good".
In stanza 4 the soul itself is likened to a "Heavenly Ey".

News from a forrein Country came,
As if my Treasure and my Wealth lay there:
    So much it did my Heart Enflame!
Twas wont to call my Soul into mine Ear.
5   Which thither went to Meet
            The Approaching Sweet:
        And on the Threshhold stood,
    To entertain the Unknown Good.
            It Hoverd there,
10   As if twould leav mine Ear.
    And was so Eager to Embrace
    The Joyfull Tidings as they came,
    Twould almost leav its Dwelling Place,
            To Entertain the Same.

15   As if the Tidings were the Things,
    My very Joys themselvs, my forrein Treasure,
        Or els did bear them on their Wings;
    With so much Joy they came, with so much Pleasure.
            My Soul stood at the Gate
20   To recreat
            It self with Bliss: And to
    Be pleasd with Speed. A fuller View
            It fain would take
            Yet Journeys back would make
25   Unto my Heart: as if twould fain
    Go out to meet, yet stay within
    To fit a place, to Entertain,
            And bring the Tidings in.

    What Sacred Instinct did inspire
30 My Soul in Childhood with a Hope so Strong?
    What Secret Force movd my Desire,
    To Expect my Joys beyond the Seas, so Yong?
            Felicity I knew
            Was out of View:
35   And being here alone,
    I saw that Happiness was gone,
            From Me! for this,

I Thirsted Absent Bliss,
And thought that sure beyond the Seas,
40   Or els in som thing near at hand
I knew not yet, (since nought did pleas
I knew.) my Bliss did stand.

But little did the Infant Dream
That all the Treasures of the World were by:
45   And that Himself was so the Cream
And Crown of all, which round about did lie.
Yet thus it was The Gem,
The Diadem,
The Ring Enclosing all
50   That Stood upon this Earthy Ball;
The Heavenly Ey,
Much Wider then the Skie,
Wher in they all included were
The Glorious Soul that was the King
55   Made to possess them, did appear
A Small and little thing!

19 *at the Gate:* of sense.

21–2 *And to . . . Speed:* and to be speedily satisfied.

32 *beyond the Seas* (and l. 39)*:* in a distant place. Cf. *Centuries III*, 24 (quoted above).

33–8 *Felicity . . . Absent Bliss:* Unlike "The Salutation", this passage suggests that the child does remember some felicity now "out of View" in this world.

37 *for:* because of.

40–56 *Or else . . . thing!:* The child does not yet perceive (since nothing which he knows satisfies his desire) that the treasure of which he has received news is near him in this world, and that of all its wonders he himself, the human creation, is the greatest. The most precious thing, "The Gem,/The Diadem", is the soul: the "Ring" or "Heavenly Ey" which, because it encloses all it sees on earth, is "Much wider then the Skie". But to his childish understanding that soul, fashioned like a king to possess all, then appeared insignificant.

SHADOWS IN THE WATER

TRAHERNE'S preoccupation with a "far distant" region existing "for other great and glorious Ends", towards which his spirit eagerly reaches and where "Som unknown Joys there be/Laid up in Store for me", is symbolized by this early recollection. Playing beside water, the child is captivated yet perplexed by the reflected country he sees there. His mistake, and the fancies and speculations evoked by it, foreshadow with unconscious wisdom a truth the adult later apprehends: the reality of the world of spirit beyond yet mirrored by that of sense, which "our second Selvs" inhabit as vividly and intensely as their material existence.

> In unexperienc'd Infancy
> Many a sweet Mistake doth ly:
> Mistake tho false, intending tru;
> A *Seeming* somwhat more than *View*;
> 5   That doth instruct the Mind
>   In Things that ly behind,
> And many Secrets to us show
> Which afterwards we com to know.
>
> Thus did I by the Water's brink
> 10   Another World beneath me think;
> And while the lofty spacious Skies
> Reversed there abus'd mine Eys,
>   I fancy'd other Feet
>   Came mine to touch and meet;
> 15   As by som Puddle I did play
> Another World within it lay.
>
> Beneath the Water Peeple drown'd,
> Yet with another Hev'n crown'd,
> In spacious Regions seem'd to go
> 20   Freely moving to and fro:
>   In bright and open Space
>   I saw their very face;

Eys, Hands, and Feet they had like mine;
Another Sun did with them shine.

25 'Twas strange that Peeple there should walk,
And yet I could not hear them talk:
That throu a little watry Chink,
Which one dry Ox or Horse might drink,
    We other Worlds should see,
30   Yet not admitted be;
And other Confines there behold
Of Light and Darkness, Heat and Cold.

I call'd them oft, but call'd in vain;
No Speeches we could entertain:
35 Yet did I there expect to find
Som other World, to pleas my Mind.
    I plainly saw by these
    A new *Antipodes*,
Whom, tho they were so plainly seen,
40 A Film kept off that stood between.

By walking Men's reversed Feet
I chanc'd another World to meet;
Tho it did not to View exceed
A Phantasm, 'tis a World indeed,
45   Where Skies beneath us shine,
    And Earth by Art divine
Another face presents below,
Where Peeple's feet against Ours go.

Within the Regions of the Air,
50 Compass'd about with Hev'ns fair,
Great Tracts of Land there may be found
Enricht with Fields and fertil Ground;
    Where many num'rous Hosts,
    In those far distant Coasts,
55 For other great and glorious Ends,
Inhabit, my yet unknown Friends.

O ye that stand upon the Brink,
Whom I so near me, throu the Chink,
With Wonder see: What Faces there,
60   Whose Feet, whose Bodies, do ye wear?
    I my Companions see
    In You, another Me.
They seemed Others, but are We;
Our second Selvs those Shadows be.

65   Look how far off those lower Skies
Extend themselvs! scarce with mine Eys
I can them reach. O ye my Friends,
What *Secret* borders on those Ends?
    Are lofty Hevens hurl'd
70   'Bout your inferior World?
    Are ye the Representatives
    Of other Peopl's distant Lives?

Of all the Play-mates which I knew
That here I do the Image view
75   In other Selvs; what can it mean?
But that below the purling Stream
        Som unknown Joys there be
        Laid up in Store for me;
To which I shall, when that thin Skin
Is broken, be admitted in.

3 *intending tru:* with a true meaning.

4 *A* Seeming . . . *View:* an intimation beyond what the bodily eye can see.

12 *abus'd:* deceived.

19–24 *In spacious Regions . . . shine:* The child's "sweet Mistake" (as also in ll. 49–52) expresses the living co-existence of the realm of spirits.

27–32 *That throu . . . Cold:* Traherne frequently marvels at the miraculous within the commonplace: here, that to the seeing eye a mere puddle can reveal "other Worlds".

38 Antipodes: a place on the opposite side of the earth.

40 *A Film:* literally of water, but also, symbolically, the barrier between sense and spirit.

44 *A Phantasm:* a phantom or illusion.

57 *the Brink:* literally of the water, symbolically of the world of spirit.

65–70 *Look . . . World?:* A paradox: the life usually envisaged "above" is seen here in physical terms of the reflected "lower Skies" and "inferior World".

73–5 *Of all . . . mean?:* i.e. What can it mean, that I view here the image in other selves of all the playmates I knew?

79 *that thin Skin:* Cf. the "Film" of l. 40: that between the world of time and sense and of eternity and spirit.

Richard Crashaw

TO THE NOBLEST & BEST OF LADYES, THE COUNTESSE OF *DENBIGH* PERSWADING HER TO RESOLUTION IN RELIGION

IT was probably after his ejection from his Cambridge Fellowship because of Royalist sympathies that Crashaw met Susan, Countess of Denbigh, First Lady of the Bedchamber to Henrietta Maria. She brought him to the notice of the Queen, who recommended him to the Pope for employment; and he dedicated to her his *Carmen Deo Nostro*, published posthumously in Paris, from "Her most devoted Servant . . . In hearty acknowledgment of his immortall obligation to her Goodnes & Charity". By 1646 Crashaw had entered the Roman Catholic Church, and in this poem he eloquently urges the Countess to follow suit (his plea, incidentally, was successful). His tone of familiar and affectionate concern for his benefactor's spiritual welfare recalls Donne's addresses to the Countess of Bedford and Lady Magdalen Herbert, and its persuasive power springs from the strength of his own conviction. L. C. Martin says that Crashaw is at his best in this poem "in the congenial task of reconciling argument, wit and poetry". Note the effectiveness of the octosyllabic couplet in achieving the epigrammatic intensity of metaphysical wit (e.g. ll. 29–30); and how the sustained metaphor of siege throughout the poem becomes explicit in the concluding paradoxes of ll. 59–68, in which the conquered will triumph and "let life in" through voluntarily yielding the victory to her opponent, Love (cf. the similar military imagery of the soul taken by storm in Donne's "Batter my heart", p. 79). Crashaw published two different versions of this poem. The first, shorter one, published in *Carmen Deo Nostro* (1652), is the text used by Grierson and given here. The longer version, printed separately in 1653, may be found in Helen Gardner's anthology, *The Metaphysical Poets*.

What heav'n-intreated HEART is This
Stands trembling at the gate of blisse;
Holds fast the door, yet dares not venture
Fairly to open it, and enter,
5 Whose DEFINITION is a Doubt
Twixt Life & Death, twixt In & Out.
Say, lingring fair! why comes the birth
Of your brave soul so slowly forth?
Plead your pretences (o you strong
10 In weaknes!) why you choose so long
In labor of your selfe to ly,
Nor daring quite to live nor dy?
Ah linger not, lov'd soul! a slow
And late consent was a long No,
15 Who grants at last, a long time tryd
And did his best to have deny'd.
What magick bolts, what mystick Barres
Maintain the will in these strange warres!
What fatall, yet fantastick, bands
20 Keep The free Heart from it's own hands!
So when the year takes cold, we see
Poor waters their owne prisoners be.
Fetter'd, & lockt up fast they ly
In a sad selfe-captivity.
25 The' astonisht nymphs their flood's strange fate deplore,
To see themselves their own severer shore.
Thou that alone canst thaw this cold,
And fetch the heart from it's strong Hold;
Allmighty LOVE! end this long warr,
30 And of a meteor make a starr.
O fix this fair INDEFINITE.
And 'mongst thy shafts of soveraign light
Choose out that sure decisive dart
Which has the Key of this close heart,
35 Knowes all the corners of't, & can controul
The self-shutt cabinet of an unsearcht soul.
O let it be at last, love's houre.

Raise this tall Trophee of thy Powre;
Come once the conquering way; not to confute
40 But kill this rebell-word, IRRESOLUTE
That so, in spite of all this peevish strength
Of weaknes, she may write RESOLV'D AT LENGTH,
Unfold at length, unfold fair flowre
And use the season of love's showre,
45 Meet his well-meaning Wounds, wise heart!
And hast to drink the wholesome dart.
That healing shaft, which heavn till now
Hath in love's quiver hid for you.
O Dart of love! arrow of light!
50 O happy you, if it hitt right,
It must not fall in vain, it must
Not mark the dry regardless dust.
Fair one, it is your fate; and brings
Æternall worlds upon it's wings.
55 Meet it with wide-spread armes; & see
It's seat your soul's just center be.
Disband dull feares; give faith the day.
To save your life, kill your delay.
It is love's seege; and sure to be
60 Your triumph, though his victory.
'Tis cowardise that keeps this feild
And want of courage not to yeild.
Yeild then, O yeild, that love may win
The Fort at last, and let life in.
65 Yeild quickly. Lest perhaps you prove
Death's prey, before the prize of love.
This Fort of your fair selfe, if't be not won,
He is repulst indeed; But you'are undone.

5–6 *Whose* DEFINITION . . . *Out:* i.e. Her heart's precise nature is defined
by its doubt, on which depends the difference between the spirit's life and
death, between *in* heaven and *out* of it.

8 *brave:* in the sense of "fine", "beautiful".

11 *labor:* birth-pangs.

13–16 *a slow . . . deny'd:* i.e. A slow and tardy consent amounts to a long denial, which ("Who") assents at last after having a long time done its best to deny the truth. (The construction of these lines is ambiguous. L. C. Martin suggests, alternatively, that they are interrogative, *viz.*: "Who can be said to grant at last when every effort has been made to combat persuasion?" George Williamson interprets them: "Delay could make a positive answer equivalent to a negative answer, if one tried and did his best to deny for a long time.")

21–6 *So when . . . shore:* The conflict between stubborn will and willing heart is likened to the waters in winter, also prisoner to their own nature when ice-bound. The nymphs (Nereids), like the heart, deplore that state which, like the will, makes "themselves their own severer shore".

30 *And . . . starr:* i.e. Fix the inconstant motion of the shooting star (meteor) into the steadfastness of the star.

34 *close:* closed.

41–2 *peevish strength . . . weaknes:* cf. ll. 9–10.

46–7 *And hast . . . shaft: hast:* haste. Cf. Joseph Beaumont (Crashaw's Cambridge friend, and thought to be the anonymous writer of the Preface to his *Steps to the Temple*): "Soft as the Ray/Of this Sweet Day/Are all his Healing Shafts where e'r they slay."

56 *It's seat . . . be:* i.e. The arrow's mark shall be your soul's true centre.

65–6 *Lest perhaps . . . love:* i.e. Lest perhaps you die before your conversion.

EASTER DAY

GRIERSON calls Crashaw a "radiant spirit", writing within a limited compass but with "two of the supreme qualities of great lyric poetry . . . ardour and music". These can be seen in this little-known poem—especially in the second stanza—published in *Steps to the Temple* (1646). The sensuous strain in Crashaw's nature sometimes betrayed him into extravagant conceits and cloying over-sweetness, but it was also the source of his soaring religious exaltation and lyrical joy. The musical and pictorial qualities of his poetry doubtless owed something to his other natural talents (mentioned by the writer of the Preface to *Steps to the Temple*) for 'Musicke, Drawing, Limning, Graving'. The flexibility of the flowing irregular lines contrasts with the tight octosyllabic couplets of the preceding poem.

Rise, Heire of fresh Eternity,
    From thy Virgin Tombe:
Rise mighty man of wonders, and thy world with thee
    Thy Tombe, the universall East,
5   Natures new wombe,
Thy Tombe, faire Immortalities perfumed Nest.

Of all the Gloryes Make Noone gay
    This is the Morne.
This rocke buds forth the fountaine of the streames of Day.
10   In joyes white Annals live this houre,
    When life was borne,
No cloud scoule on his radiant lids no tempest lowre.

Life, by this light's Nativity
    All creatures have.
15 Death onely by this Dayes just Doome is forc't to Dye;
    Nor is Death forc't; for may hee ly
    Thron'd in thy Grave;
Death will on this condition be content to Dy.

---

4 *Thy Tombe . . . East:* Christ's tomb becomes through the Resurrection the East (place of the sun's rising) for all men.

5-6 *Natures new wombe . . . Nest:* The place of death is transformed into the new one of birth and the source of immortality (the nest is a favourite image in Crashaw's poems).

9 *This rocke:* the tomb.

10 *live this houre:* may this hour live.

12 *his:* joy's.

13-14 *Life . . . have:* i.e. All creatures have life by the birth of this light of Easter Day.

15-18 *Death onely . . . Dy:* The metaphysical conceit of Death as the only victim of the Resurrection recalls the conclusion of Donne's Holy Sonnet "Death be not proud":

      One short sleepe past, wee wake eternally,
      And death shall be no more, Death thou shalt die.

Andrew Marvell

THE CORONET

In his religious poetry Marvell generally employs more elaborate technical devices than in the plainer style of his secular verse. Form and content are consciously fused in this religious pastoral "set with Skill and chosen out with Care", in which the patterns of rhyme and metre combine to trace both the intricate weaving of the chaplet and the "winding Snare" of the Serpent entwined among its flowers. In one sense Marvell's concern is with the problem of writing religious poetry. His shepherd, repenting of his earlier profane songs, resolves to make amends by fashioning a fitting tribute in words for "the king of Glory", but is forced to recognize the inadequacy of his art, however lovingly wrought, for this task; for implicit in the very care bestowed on the making of the "coronet" is the hope of fame, the taint of self-interest. In a larger context, however, the theme is one of sin and salvation: the inevitability for man of self-deception and the insidious snare of pride (symbolized by the Serpent), the impossibility of the pure, unmixed motive. The "curious frame" of l. 22, which must if necessary be "shattered" in order to destroy the ancient tempter, is at once the cunningly contrived artifice of the poem itself, represented by the coronet, and the complex, fallible human creature, such a mixture of the well-intentioned and the worldly, who has composed it. Only when it is "disentangled" from the debasement of "mortal Glory", and imperfection trampled underfoot by the One who alone can untie the "slipp'ry knots" of the Serpent, can the wreath of flowers become a "chaplet" in the word's other sense of a small rosary—a prayer of disinterested and selfless love of God. With its concentrated richness of simultaneous meanings which spring from the central conceit and lead to the paradoxical wit of the closing couplet, Marvell's dramatization of conversion and the progress from pride to a final humility recalls many of Herbert's poems. (It is particularly reminiscent

of "A Wreath", in which the poet, offering his "wreathed garland of
deserved praise" to God, deplores his own "deceit" and "crooked winding
wayes" and pleads for "simplicitie"—that purity of motive which is
Marvell's aspiration too.) The volume on Marvell edited by Michael
Wilding for Macmillan's "Modern Judgements" series (1969) contains
on pp. 233–48 an illuminating extended discussion of this poem by John
E. Hardy.

> When for the Thorns with which I long, too long,
>> With many a piercing wound,
>> My Saviours head have crown'd,
> I seek with Garlands to redress that Wrong:
> 5   Through every Garden, every Mead,
> I gather flow'rs (my fruits are only flow'rs)
>> Dismantling all the fragrant Towers
> That once adorned my Shepherdesses head.
> And now when I have summ'd up all my store,
> 10   Thinking (so I my self deceive)
>> So rich a Chaplet thence to weave
> As never yet the king of Glory wore:
>> Alas I find the Serpent old
>> That, twining in his speckled breast,
> 15   About the flow'rs disguis'd does fold,
>> With wreaths of Fame and Interest.
> Ah, foolish Man, that would'st debase with them,
> And mortal Glory, Heaven's Diadem!
> But thou who only could'st the Serpent tame,
> 20 Either his slipp'ry knots at once untie,
> And disintangle all his winding Snare:
> Or shatter too with him my curious frame:
> And let these wither, so that he may die,
> Though set with Skill and chosen out with Care.
> 25 That they, while Thou on both their Spoils dost tread,
> May crown thy Feet, that could not crown thy Head.

1 *the Thorns:* his sins in general as well as his pagan love poems.

6 (*my fruits are only flow'rs*): Cf. *Matt.* vii, 20: "Wherefore by their fruits
ye shall know them." The speaker's have hitherto never matured from the

implicitly frivolous and decorative stage of flowers: an admission of spiritual
inadequacy which, increasing through the poem, suggests that they can do
so only through the divine grace he is seeking.

7–8 *Dismantling . . . head:* i.e. renouncing all my former worldly pleasures
and pastimes. A "tower" was a fashionable high decorated head-dress worn
by women in the seventeenth century; his "shepherdess" symbolizes profane
love, and the "fragrant Towers", the songs written to celebrate it.

13 *the Serpent old:* the tempter of Eden.

14 *twining in:* entwining.

16 *wreaths:* the Serpent's coils concealed in the flowery wreath.

22 *curious:* intricately wrought

23 *these:* i.e. the meretricious flowers of his poetic eloquence blemished
by self-interest.

25 *both their Spoils:* i.e. the temptations of the Serpent and the pride and
debased motives of the poet.

26 *May crown . . . Head:* Cf. a similar paradox in the closing couplet of
Crashaw, "The Weeper": "Crown'd heads are Toyes; We goe to meete/
A worthy object: Our Lord's Feet."

ON A DROP OF DEW

As there are various echoes of Cowley in Marvell's two poems in the first
section (pp. 69–73), this religious meditation clearly shows the influence
of another of his Cambridge contemporaries, Crashaw, in both thought and
imagery. Marvell's Platonic aspiration towards purity and the soul's
yearning for the place of its origin is expressed through a sustained metaphysical conceit. The first part of the poem describes the natural activity
and imagined feelings of a drop of dew, finally drawn up by the sun to the
sky; and the second half, the spiritual activity it has been used to symbolize,
of the soul drawn up by God to heaven. The complexity of the rhyme-
scheme and the metrical variety in lines of four, six, seven, eight and ten
syllables show a greater freedom and flexibility of form than the regular
octosyllables of much of Marvell's work. The final four lines, coming after
the shorter ones which precede them, give an impressive measured emphasis
to the conclusion.

> See how the Orient Dew,
> Shed from the Bosom of the Morn

Into the blowing Roses,
Yet careless of its Mansion new,
5   For the clear Region where 'twas born,
Round in its self incloses,
And in its little Globes Extent,
Frames as it can its native Element.
How it the purple flow'r does slight,
10   Scarce touching where it lyes,
But gazing back upon the Skies,
Shines with a mournful Light;
Like its own Tear,
Because so long divided from the Sphear.
15   Restless it roules and unsecure,
Trembling lest it grow impure:
Till the warm Sun pitty it's Pain,
And to the Skies exhale it back again.
So the Soul, that Drop, that Ray
20   Of the clear Fountain of Eternal Day,
Could it within the humane flow'r be seen,
Remembring still its former height,
Shuns the sweet leaves and blossoms green;
And, recollecting its own Light,
25   Does, in its pure and circling thoughts, express
The greater Heaven in an Heaven less.
In how coy a Figure wound,
Every way it turns away:
So the World excluding round,
30   Yet receiving in the Day.
Dark beneath, but bright above:
Here disdaining, there in Love,
How loose and easie hence to go:
How girt and ready to ascend.
35   Moving but on a point below,
It all about does upwards bend.
Such did the Manna's sacred Dew destil;
White, and intire, though congeal'd and chill.
Congeal'd on Earth: but does, dissolving, run
40   Into the Glories of th' Almighty Sun.

1 *Orient:* eastern.

3 *the blowing Roses:* These correspond to "the humane flow'r", the body (l. 21).

4–8 *Yet careless . . . native Element:* i.e. Yet indifferent to its new home, because of ("For") the sky where it was born, encloses itself in its own orb and in that compass contains, as it can, "its native Element", heaven (cf. l. 26).

9 *the purple flow'r:* the object of "slight". "Purple" then usually meant "crimson" (cf. Donne's "Hymn to God my God, in my sicknesse", l. 26 and footnote).

13 *Like its own Tear:* Cf. Crashaw, "Wishes to his (supposed) Mistresse", l. 51: "bee its own Teare".

14 *the Sphear:* In Ptolemaic astronomy the sky was the heavenly sphere.

18 *exhale it back again:* evaporate it.

19–20 *So the Soul . . . Eternal Day:* The drop of moisture becomes a ray of light by way of "the clear fountain". Cf. Crashaw, "Easter Day", l. 9 (p. 135).

22 *Remembring . . . height:* Cf. the similar thought in Vaughan, "The Retreate", especially ll. 9–10 (p. 119), and in Traherne, "On News", ll. 33–8 (pp. 125–6).

23 *blossoms green:* H. M. Margoliouth notes that Marvell uses "green", one of his favourite adjectives, no less than twenty-five times in the 1681 volume of his *Miscellaneous Poems.*

24 *recollecting:* collecting again.

27 *coy:* modest.

29 *So . . . round:* Thus excluding, shutting out, the world on every side.

30 *the Day:* Cf. l. 20.

31–2 *Dark . . . Love:* i.e. dark on earth, which it disdains, but bright turned towards heaven, where it is "in Love".

34 *girt:* girded, prepared.

36 *upwards bend:* Cf. Herbert, "The Flower", l. 30 (p. 96).

37–40 *Such did . . . Sun:* Cf. *Exodus* xvi, 13–21: "And when the dew that lay was gone up, behold, upon the face of the wilderness there lay a small round thing, as small as the hoar frost on the ground. . . . And they gathered it morning by morning . . . and when the sun waxed hot it melted."

40 *th' Almighty Sun:* Marvell puns on the word "Sun" in the same way as Donne does in "A Hymne to God the Father", l. 15 (p. 85).

EYES AND TEARS

THIS poem too is much indebted to Crashaw, in particular to his long poem "The Weeper", which Leishman feels "almost certainly suggested" it; "and the fourteen stanzas into which its fifty-six octosyllabic couplets are divided are as loosely connected and as transposable as those of Crashaw's poem, each of them developing, more cerebrally and definingly and less pictorially than Crashaw, some ingenious metaphor or simile to express the superiority of tears to any other terrestrial sight and of sorrow to any other human emotion" (*Proceedings of the British Academy*, XLVII, 1961, reprinted in *Marvell: Modern Judgements*, ed. Wilding). The subject of tears was a favourite one in seventeenth-century poetry (see headnote to Crashaw's "Upon the Death of a Gentleman", p. 59); and Marvell's central idea is indeed a variation of that in Crashaw's poem, of tears being more eloquent than words. The theme which emerges from this multiplicity of diverse similitudes is *lacrimae rerum*, the tears at the heart of things: "the true price of all . . . Joyes" to which the fairest prizes of life, even man's laughter and the pleasures of "every Garden", turn in the end, while the "all-seeing" sun itself, distilling the essence of the world, finds it "only Showers" and in compassion pours them back. From his opening praise of the wisdom of nature in making the eyes the organ of both grief and sight, however, Marvell expands a further concept of tears, as the necessary corrective to the vanity of human experience viewed by "the Self-deluding Sight". Measuring its errors through the employment (as in "The Definition of Love") of geometrical imagery—the angle, the plumb-line, the weighing scales— he sees them lend a sadder but juster perspective, which is communicated by conjuring up an almost bewildering succession of crowding images. Because the function of tears is "to preserve [the] Sight more true", weeping is the "noblest Use" of the eyes. Only when their faculties are transposed— eyes washed to clarity by weeping, tears assuming the ability to see—so that the two are fused into one, can the human vision of life be perfected and complete.

> How wisely Nature did decree,
> With the same Eyes to weep and see!
> That, having view'd the object vain,
> They might be ready to complain.

5   And, since the Self-deluding Sight,
     In a false Angle takes each hight;
     These Tears which better measure all,
     Like wat'ry Lines and Plummets fall.

     Two Tears, which Sorrow long did weigh
10   Within the Scales of either Eye,
     And then paid out in equal Poise,
     Are the true price of all my Joyes.

     What in the World most fair appears,
     Yea even Laughter, turns to Tears:
15   And all the Jewels which we prize,
     Melt in these Pendants of the Eyes.

     I have through every Garden been,
     Amongst the Red, the White, the Green;
     And yet, from all the flow'rs I saw,
20   No Hony, but these Tears could draw.

     So the all-seeing Sun each day
     Distills the World with Chymick Ray;
     But finds the Essence only Showers,
     Which straight in pity back he powers.

25   Yet happy they whom Grief doth bless,
     That weep the more, and see the less:
     And, to preserve their Sight more true,
     Bathe still their Eyes in their own Dew.

     So *Magdalen*, in Tears more wise
30   Dissolv'd those captivating Eyes,
     Whose liquid Chaines could flowing meet
     To fetter her Redeemers feet.

     Not full sailes hasting loaden home,
     Nor the chast Ladies pregnant Womb,
35   Nor *Cynthia* Teeming show's so fair,
     As two Eyes swoln with weeping are.

     The sparkling Glance that shoots Desire,
     Drench'd in these Waves, does lose its fire.

Yea oft the Thund'rer pitty takes
40 And here the hissing Lightning slakes.

The Incense was to Heaven dear,
Not as a Perfume, but a Tear.
And Stars shew lovely in the Night,
But as they seem the Tears of Light.

45 Ope then mine Eyes your double Sluice,
And practise so your noblest Use.
For others too can see, or sleep;
But only humane Eyes can weep.

Now like two Clouds dissolving, drop,
50 And at each Tear in distance stop:
Now like two Fountains trickle down:
Now like two floods o'return and drown.

Thus let your Streams o'reflow your Springs,
Till Eyes and Tears be the same things:
55 And each the other's difference bears;
These weeping Eyes, those seeing Tears.

29–32 *So* Magdalen . . . *feet:* Leishman observes that this stanza "might almost be regarded as a complimentary allusion to Crashaw's weeping Magdalene".

34–6 *Nor the chast Ladies . . . weeping are:* In this almost voluptuous pleasure in the contemplation of grief Marvell here, too, strongly recalls Crashaw.

35 Cynthia *Teeming:* the full moon.

37–8 *The sparkling Glance . . . fire:* i.e. Sexual desire is quenched in tears—an idea which is linked to the subduing of profane to divine love in ll. 29–32.

39 *the Thund'rer:* Jupiter, who often slakes his heat in tears—i.e. rain.

41–2 *The Incense . . . Tear:* i.e. The "incense" of prayer is more prized by heaven if it springs not from mere ritual but repentance.

43–4 *And Stars . . . Light:* i.e. Stars are beautiful not only as natural phenomena but for their religious significance as tears shed from the light of eternity.

48 *But . . . weep:* See, however, ll. 95–100 of Marvell's "The Nymph complaining for the death of her Faun", in which the dying creature weeps.

A DIALOGUE BETWEEN THE SOUL AND BODY

DONNE's preoccupation with the relation between body and soul in sexual love is here explored by Marvell in the wider context of the whole of human life. Donne invariably upholds the Aristotelian view of the union of body and soul in man, with each necessary and complementary to the other (as in, for example, ll. 53–6 of "The Exstasie"). Traherne too believed that the senses and bodily faculties act as the soul's allies, bringing man news of a world beyond this one which kindles the desire of his spirit; thus making the body a bridge between the visible finite beauty which delights it and the invisible and infinite which is made manifest in creation (see notes to "The Salutation", "On News", and "Shadows in the Water", pp. 122–30). Marvell presents here the opposite, Platonic, doctrine of the soul imprisoned in the flesh (see Helen Gardner's comment in the footnote to "The Exstasie", l. 68, pp. 28–9). He shows body and soul as intrinsically inimical and in perpetual conflict: the one cramped and confined in its "dungeon" of flesh and bone, the other "impaled" in equal bondage by a tyrant who torments it with restlessness and painful emotions which, paradoxically, fit it for, rather than keep it from, sin. Yet Marvell also recognizes the difficulty, even the final impossibility, of making that clear-cut distinction between the two which his title and opening lines suggest; and therein lies the subtle ambivalence of this dialogue of mutual complaint. "A vain Head, and double Heart" are attributed by the soul to the body; yet these are more than mere material organs of the physical being (the heart's "double" function is plainly stated in the epithet), and partake in the activity of the soul. In the same way the soul cannot divorce itself from the body's "griefs" of sickness: "I feel, that cannot feel, the pain"—while the body likewise suffers the soul's maladies of passions which "Physick yet could never reach". As the poem proceeds it becomes increasingly apparent that, however unwillingly and for all the limitations and constraints which each imposes on the other, body and soul are truly interdependent. The complexity of the human organism in which each is inextricably involved in the experience of the other defies the simple antithesis and dichotomy originally implied.

Soul

O who shall, from this Dungeon, raise
A Soul inslav'd so many wayes?

With bolts of Bones, that fetter'd stands
In Feet; and manacled in Hands.
5   Here blinded with an Eye; and there
Deaf with the drumming of an Ear.
A Soul hung up, as 'twere, in Chains
Of Nerves, and Arteries, and Veins.
Tortur'd, besides each other part,
10 In a vain Head, and double Heart.

Body

O who shall me deliver whole,
From bonds of this Tyrannic Soul?
Which, stretcht upright, impales me so,
That mine own Precipice I go;
15 And warms and moves this needless Frame:
(A Fever could but do the same.)
And, wanting where its spight to try,
Has made me live to let me dye.
A Body that could never rest,
20 Since this ill Spirit it possest.

Soul

What Magick could me thus confine
Within anothers Grief to pine?
Where whatsoever it complain,
I feel, that cannot feel, the pain.
25 And all my Care its self employes,
That to preserve, which me destroys:
Constrain'd not only to indure
Diseases, but, whats worse, the Cure:
And ready oft the Port to gain,
30 Am Shipwrackt into Health again.

Body

But Physick yet could never reach
The Maladies Thou me dost teach;
Whom first the Cramp of Hope does Tear:

And then the Palsie Shakes of Fear.
35 The Pestilence of Love does heat:
Or Hatred's hidden Ulcer eat.
Joy's chearful Madness does perplex:
Or Sorrow's other Madness vex.
Which Knowledge forces me to know;
40 And Memory will not foregoe.
What but a Soul could have the wit
To build me up for Sin so fit?
So Architects do square and hew
Green Trees that in the Forest grew.

3–8 *With bolts . . . Veins:* This precisely detailed anatomical imagery would have appealed to the keen contemporary interest in the mechanism of the human body (see Introduction, p. 2). It is interesting to contrast Marvell's idea in ll. 5–6 of the soul's being blinded and deafened by eye and ear with Traherne's in "On News", where the soul is compared to a "Heavenly Ey" and the ear acts as the messenger bringing it tidings of an "Unknown Good". It epitomises the difference between puritan asceticism and Traherne's self-styled "Christian epicureanism".

10 *double Heart:* i.e. serving two masters—the body in its physical function and the soul in its non-material one. The adjective also carries the undertone of "double-dealing", "deceiving".

13–14 *Which, stretcht . . . go:* cf. Marvell's *Rehearsal Transpros'd*, i, 64: "After he was stretch'd to such an height in his own fancy, that he could not look down from top to toe but his Eyes dazled at the Precipice of his Stature". The image corresponds to the soul's complaint (l. 7) of being "hung up . . . in Chains".

15 *this needless Frame:* i.e. which until it was animated by the soul had no wants or needs, and was content to be so.

17–18 *And, wanting . . . dye:* i.e. seeking how to vent its spite, has given the body life (and awareness of the fact of death) only that it may finally die.

19–20 *A Body . . . possest:* Another variation on the theme of human restlessness (cf. "The Pulley", p. 98, and Vaughan's "Man", pp. 113–14). Here the body lays the blame for it on the soul.

26 *That . . . destroys:* As long as the body is preserved the soul continues to languish in its "dungeon".

29–30 *And ready . . . again:* i.e. Often prepared for its release by the body's sickness and expected death, the soul is thwarted by its recovery.

41–4 *What but . . . grew:* Without the soul the body, as a part of nature, would not have the capacity to sin. The characteristic concluding image draws the analogy between the world to which the body belongs, the green trees in the forest, and the civilizing "architect" soul which destroys nature in its desire to build something of its own creation.

BERMUDAS

THIS poem, like many of Donne's, reflects the contemporary interest in distant and recently discovered lands. The Bermudas, discovered by Juan Bermudez in 1515, were also known as the "Summer", or "Somers", Islands, after Sir George Somers who had been wrecked there in 1609. Marvell's poem was probably written in or about 1653, when he went to Eton as tutor to Cromwell's ward William Dutton and lived in the house of the Rev. John Oxenbridge, a Fellow of the College, who had sailed for the Bermudas nearly twenty years earlier in order to escape religious persecution. This would have suggested the theme of the prodigal bounty of nature towards the English pilgrims on an island "far kinder than [their] own", where there was safety from the "Storms" of both civil strife and "Prelat's rage". Yet the emigrants' exultant song, to which the rhythm of their rowing keeps time, is on a "holy" as well as a "chearful Note"; for they recognize and give thanks for a deliverance which is due to the benevolence of the Provider who has guided them here and who dispenses for their benefit the beauty and plenty of the island, with the freedom to worship in such a place. This is an exile where all nature is subservient to the needs of man, and is indeed almost domesticated by his arrival (the shore "a grassy Stage", the images of enamel and jewels, the oranges like "golden Lamps" and the rocks forming a "Temple"). For his pictorial evocation of the landscape (which recalls the attraction for him of the exotic scene glimpsed in ll. 5–6 of "To his Coy Mistress") Marvell probably drew upon the descriptions in Captain John Smith's *The Generall Historie of Virginia, New England and the Summer Isles* (1624). Cf. also Waller, "Battle of the Summer Islands" (1645), i, ll. 6–11, in which he describes:

> That happy island where huge lemons grow,
> And orange trees, which golden fruit do bear,
> The Hesperian garden boasts of none so fair;
> Where shining pearl, coral, and many a pound,

On the rich shore, of ambergris is found.
The lofty cedar . . .

The directness and simplicity of the octosyllabic couplets in this "fine poem",
as Lamb called it (and for which Tennyson too had "special praise"),
are entirely appropriate to their subject of the Puritan emigration.

Where the remote *Bermudas* ride
In th' Oceans bosome unespy'd,
From a small Boat, that row'd along,
The listning Winds receiv'd this Song.
5   What should we do but sing his Praise
That led us through the watry Maze,
Unto an Isle so long unknown,
And yet far kinder than our own?
Where he the huge Sea-Monsters wracks,
10   That lift the Deep upon their Backs.
He lands us on a grassy Stage;
Safe from the Storms, and Prelat's rage.
He gave us this eternal Spring,
Which here enamells every thing;
15   And sends the Fowls to us in care,
On daily Visits through the Air.
He hangs in shades the Orange bright,
Like golden Lamps in a green Night.
And does in the Pomgranates close,
20   Jewels more rich than *Ormus* shows.
He makes the Figs our mouths to meet;
And throws the Melons at our feet.
But Apples plants of such a price,
No Tree could ever bear them twice.
25   With Cedars, chosen by his hand,
From *Lebanon*, he stores the Land.
And makes the hollow Seas, that roar,
Proclaime the Ambergris on shoar.
He cast (of which we rather boast)
30   The Gospels Pearl upon our Coast.
And in these Rocks for us did frame

A Temple, where to sound his Name.
Oh let our Voice his Praise exalt,
Till it arrive at Heavens Vault:
35 Which thence (perhaps) rebounding, may
Eccho beyond the *Mexique Bay*.
Thus sung they, in the *English* boat,
An holy and a chearful Note,
And all the way, to guide their Chime,
40 With falling Oars they kept the time.

9–10 *Where he . . . Backs:* In Waller's poem (above) the "battle" described is between the inhabitants and two stranded whales. Here God "wrecks" the whales like ships.

13 *He gave . . . Spring:* In his *Historie* (p. 170) John Smith observes that "There seemes to be a continuall Spring . . . and though the trees shed their leaves, yet they are alwaies full of greene." Waller (who may also have used this source) says (i, ll. 40–1): "For the kind spring, which but salutes us here,/ Inhabits there, and courts them all the year".

20 Ormus: Hormuz, on the Persian Gulf.

21–2 *He makes . . . feet:* Cf. Marvell's "The Garden", ll. 33–6 and 39: "What wond'rous Life in this I lead!/Ripe Apples drop about my head;/ The Luscious Clusters of the Vine/Upon my Mouth do crush their Wine . . ./ Stumbling on Melons, as I pass . . ."

23–4 *But Apples . . . twice:* i.e. pineapples, which the colonists had introduced into the Bermudas.

28 *Ambergris:* a fragrant grey waxy substance excreted by the sperm whale, found on tropical shores and used in perfumery.

29–30 *He cast . . . Coast:* They dare to "boast" because it is through their endeavours and privations that the "pearl" of the Gospel (cf. Waller, above, l. 9: "shining pearl") has been brought to these shores.

36 Mexique Bay: The Bay of Mexico.

Select Bibliography

The Poems of John Donne, edited by Herbert J. C. Grierson, 2 vols. Oxford: Clarendon Press, 1912.

John Donne: The Divine Poems, edited by Helen Gardner. Oxford: Clarendon Press, 1952.

John Donne: The Elegies and The Songs and Sonnets, edited by Helen Gardner. Oxford: Clarendon Press, 1965.

The Works of George Herbert, edited by F. E. Hutchinson. Oxford: Clarendon Press, 1941.

The Poems of Richard Crashaw, edited by L. C. Martin. Oxford: Clarendon Press, 1927 (2nd edn. 1957).

The Poems and Letters of Andrew Marvell, edited by H. M. Margoliouth, 2 vols. Oxford: Clarendon Press, 1927 (2nd edn. 1952).

The Works of Henry Vaughan, edited by L. C. Martin. Oxford: Clarendon Press, 1914 (2nd edn. 1957).

Thomas Traherne: Centuries, Poems and Thanksgivings, edited by H. M. Margoliouth, 2 vols. Oxford: Clarendon Press, 1958.

Metaphysical Lyrics and Poems of the Seventeenth Century, edited by Herbert J. C. Grierson. Oxford: Clarendon Press, 1921.

The Metaphysical Poets, edited by Helen Gardner. Oxford: Clarendon Press, 1957; 2nd edn. 1967 (also available in a Penguin edition).

Four Metaphysical Poets (Donne, Herbert, Vaughan, Crashaw), by Joan Bennett. Cambridge, 1934. Revised, 1964, under the title *Five Metaphysical Poets*, with the addition of a chapter on Marvell.